THE
ENCYCLOPAEDIA
OF
SEWING
TECHNIQUES

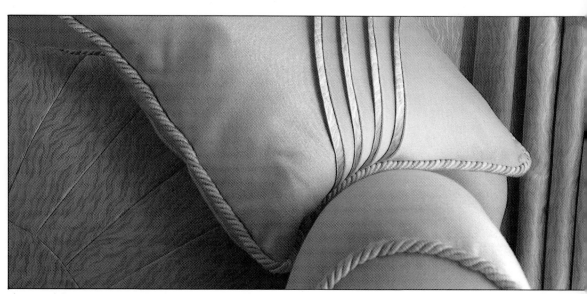

Photograph by Interior Selection Ltd.

THE

ENCYCLOPAEDIA

OF

SEWING

TECHNIQUES

JAN EATON

GUILD PUBLISHING LONDON

A QUARTO BOOK

This edition Published 1986
by arrangement with
Book Club Associates

Published in 1986 by
Hamlyn Publishing
A division of The Hamlyn Publishing Group Ltd
Bridge House, London Road,
Twickenham, Middlesex, England

This book was designed and produced by
Quarto Publishing Ltd
The Old Brewery, 6 Blundell Street
London N7 9BH

Senior Editor: Helen Owen
Editor: Jane Laing
Art Editor: Hazel Edington
Designer: Richard Mellor
Design Assistant: Ursula Dawson
Illustrator: Mary Horner
Photographer: John Heseltine
Indexer: Richard Bird
Art Director: Peter Laws
Editorial Director: Jim Miles

Typeset by Burbeck Associates Limited, Harlow, Essex
Manufactured in Hong Kong by
Regent Publishing Services Limited
Printed by Leefung-Asco Printers Limited, Hong Kong

C O N T E N T S

C O N T E N T S

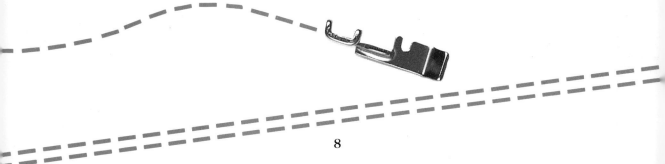

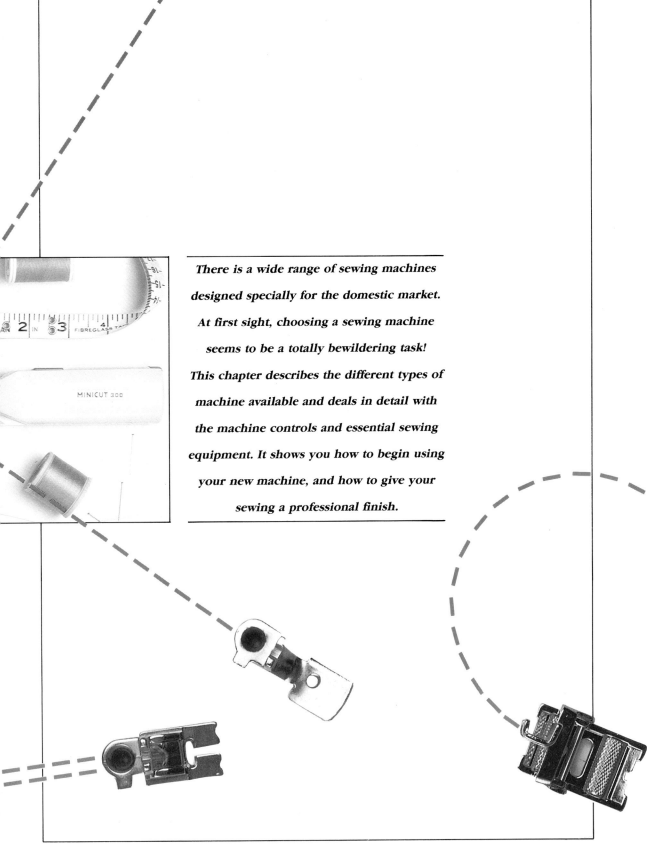

There is a wide range of sewing machines
designed specially for the domestic market.
At first sight, choosing a sewing machine
seems to be a totally bewildering task!
This chapter describes the different types of
machine available and deals in detail with
the machine controls and essential sewing
equipment. It shows you how to begin using
your new machine, and how to give your
sewing a professional finish.

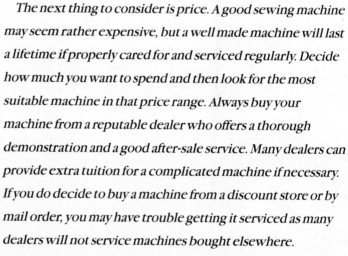

C H O O S I N G   A   S E W I N G   M A C H I N E

A simple zigzag machine with a free arm, semi-automatic buttonhole and a choice of stretch stitches will be adequate for most dressmaking and home sewing needs. A heavier type of machine with good needle penetration and a slow stitch control would be better for heavy fabrics and tailoring processes. If you have to pack your machine away after each sewing session, choose a portable, lightweight model which is easy to lift. Machines with sensitive knee or push button controls are available for users who cannot cope with a conventional foot control. Other machines have a range of decorative features, but they will be much more expensive. It is worth remembering that no single machine will encompass all the features on offer by the different manufacturers, so you must choose which features are essential to you.

SEWING MACHINES

The first step when choosing a sewing machine is to decide which type of machine will suit your particular needs, as they fall into quite distinct categories.

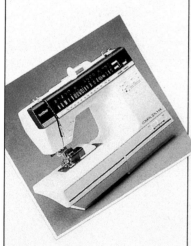

The next thing to consider is price. A good sewing machine may seem rather expensive, but a well made machine will last a lifetime if properly cared for and serviced regularly. Decide how much you want to spend and then look for the most suitable machine in that price range. Always buy your machine from a reputable dealer who offers a thorough demonstration and a good after-sale service. Many dealers can provide extra tuition for a complicated machine if necessary. If you do decide to buy a machine from a discount store or by mail order, you may have trouble getting it serviced as many dealers will not service machines bought elsewhere.

Try out as many machines as you can that look suitable, using scraps of your own fabric. Take along a selection of different weights and types of fabric, including a thin, slippery synthetic and a stretchy knit as these can be difficult to sew on some machines. Stitch through double fabric and check that the machine stitches evenly without allowing the fabric to 'creep' under the foot. Ask the demonstrator to show you the stretch stitches and those for neatening raw edges. Try out the threading and bobbin winding procedures for ease of use. Other features to look at include the position of the light, which should be directly over the needle, the instruction book and also the response of the foot or knee control.

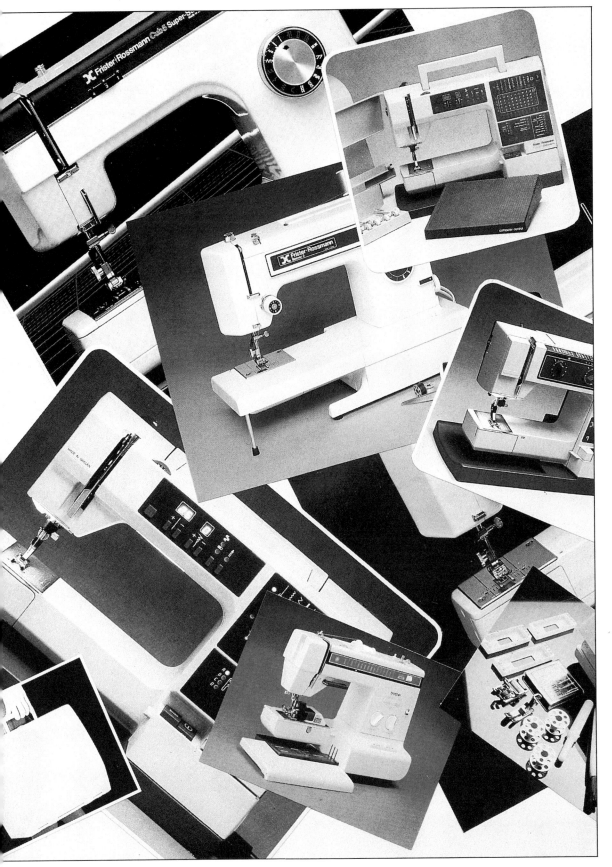

TYPES OF MACHINE

STRAIGHT STITCH

These are the simplest type of machine available and now made by very few manufacturers. These machines sew varying lengths of straight stitch forwards or in reverse and, although very limited in scope, are extremely reliable. They have a flat bed around the stitching area to provide support for the fabric.

BASIC ZIGZAG

These machines have a simple swing needle facility, which will sew an adjustable zigzag stitch up to 5mm (¼in) wide as well as a straight stitch. The zigzag stitch can be closed up for satin stitch and buttonholes that have to be worked by pivoting the fabric and adjusting the stitch width manually. Straight stitching can usually be done with the needle at the right, centre or left of the foot. These machines either have a flat bed or a free arm, which is useful when stitching openings and small circular areas such as sleeves and cuffs. There are controls for stitch length, stitch width, a push button reverse and also a limited range of feet and attachments.

SEMI-AUTOMATIC

Semi-automatic machines have more useful features than the basic zigzag type and they can also do simple decorative stitches. They have straight and zigzag stitch facilities, variable needle positions, push button reverse and stitch length and width controls. In addition they have pattern cams which alter the width control automatically to form simple, decorative stitches based on satin stitch. The pattern cams are either inserted manually inside the machine or selected by a knob or lever on the outside. The patterns are based on geometric and curved shapes and they can be worked on a close satin stitch setting or opened up by use of the stitch length lever. These machines also offer a semi-automatic buttonhole. The fabric still has to be pivoted manually, but the width of the satin stitch is pre-set by turning a dial. They also have a wider range of feet and attachments and are available as either flat-bed or free-arm models.

AUTOMATIC

The definition of an automatic sewing machine is one which has a built-in automatic buttonhole, which can be stitched without pivoting the fabric. The button-hole is worked in two, four or five steps and the width of the satin stitch is pre-set. This definition means that a machine with an automatic buttonhole and a few utility stitches comes into the same category as a machine with many more advanced features such as automatic patterns and trimotion stitches for stretch fabric. With the advanced machines, the fabric is moved backwards and forwards beneath the needle and the needle bar may move from side to side as well, depending on the automatic stitch selected. This gives a range of stretch and overlock utility stitches and a large choice of decorative stitches. New models of this type wind the bobbin through the needle to save unthreading the machine.

ELECTRONIC

Electronic machines have all the features of the advanced auto-matic machines, including mechanical pattern cams, but by the use of electronics they make the physical process of stitching easier. They have an integrated circuit located either in the machine or in the foot control, which controls the mechanical functions. Some machines use both a circuit in the machine and one in the foot control. An electronic foot control regulates the speed of the motor and provides full needle power even at slow speeds or when stitching heavyweight fabric. It allows more sensitive control and the ability to stop and start immediately. The circuit in the machine provides for stitch-by-stitch sewing, allow-ing the machine to stop with the needle either up or down. Some electronic machines dis-pense with a foot control altogether and the machine operations are controlled by various push buttons. This type of machine is ideal if you have difficulty using a foot control.

COMPUTERIZED

These are the most sophisticated machines available and they are controlled by a built-in micro-processor. They have a full range of features including a one-step buttonhole, but their real advantage is their wide range of decorative options. There are no mechanically operated pattern cams, as the stitch patterns are stored in the computer memory. The stitch patterns are chosen by touching a button and the selection is then shown on a visual display panel. Pre-programmed motifs and al-phabets can be elongated or shortened without losing the density of the stitches and they can be inverted or stitched in mirror image. A sequence of stitch patterns can be chosen and dialled into the machine, which will then repeat the sequence exactly.

M A C H I N E   C O N T R O L S

Machine controls may look different from machine to machine but their basic functions are the same. All sewing machines require a continuous thread to be fed to the needle at the correct tension and connected to a second tensioned thread from the bobbin. These two threads form the lock stitch, which is the basis of all machine stitches. The thread spindle, located on the top of the machine, holds the reel of thread for the needle and allows it to unwind evenly. Some machines have more than one spindle to allow twin and triple needles to be used.

Thread Guide

Tension Disc

Machine Foot

Needleplate

BOBBIN WINDER

The bobbin winding position differs according to the machine, but the thread always passes through a tension control to ensure even winding. The balance wheel is disengaged in order to wind the bobbin. Many machines have an automatic cut-off feature when the bobbin is full and on some sophisticated machines the bobbin can be wound directly through the needle without unthreading.

BALANCE WHEEL

The machine is worked by turning the balance wheel which is usually driven by an electric motor. The balance wheel can be turned by hand to make a single stitch or to raise and lower the needle.

FOOT CONTROLS

Foot controls can be electric, electronic or worked by air pressure control.

MACHINE FEET

All machines, except the straight stitch type, have at least two feet provided with them, one for straight stitch and one for zigzag. Some machines have a selection of special purpose feet which come as standard, while others have a range which can be purchased separately. The feet are hinged to accommodate different weights of fabric, and they can be screwed in place or clipped on to a shank.

Bobbin Winder

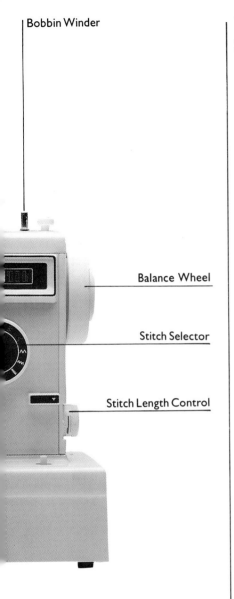

Balance Wheel

Stitch Selector

Stitch Length Control

NEEDLE

The needle is fixed into the needle bar by a small screw which should be tightened firmly after inserting the needle.

PRESSER BAR

The presser bar holds the machine foot and often in-corporates a thread cutter at the back of the bar. The pressure can be adjusted to suit different weights of fabric.

PRESSER BAR LIFTER

This is a lever positioned behind and above the foot which raises and lowers the foot. The thread tension is engaged only when the foot is lowered.

BOBBINS AND BOBBIN CASES

Bobbins are circular and vary in size according to the machine, so they are not usually interchangeable. The bobbin thread feeds through a tension spring on the bobbin case which can be adjusted. The bobbin fits snugly into the bobbin case which either slots in under the needleplate or is inserted from the side.

STITCH SELECTOR

If the machine features a few utility and pattern stitches, the controls are usually incorporated into the stitch width dial, which will be marked with the appropriate symbols. Automatic machines have a pattern panel with a lever or movable pointer which selects the stitches.

TAKE-UP LEVER AND THREAD GUIDES

The thread feeds though the eye in the take-up lever and down to the needle. Thread guides are small loops of wire which guide the thread from the reel to the needle. Some machines have a slotted take-up lever and thread guides to make threading quick and simple.

STITCH LENGTH CONTROL

The length of stitch is determined by the rate at which the fabric is fed under the foot. This feeding mechanism is called the feed dog and is regulated by the stitch length control. This control can be a lever with graduated markings or a numbered dial. The feed dog can be dropped on most machines for darning and free embroidery.

STITCH WIDTH CONTROL

This control is found on all machines except the straight stitch type. It controls the width of the zigzag and decorative stitches and may be a graduated lever or a numbered dial. Some machines have a dial or lever marked left, middle and right, which allows the needle to be set in one of these positions.

TENSION DISCS

Tension discs are situated on the front of the machine or partially concealed on the top. They act like brakes and control the rate at which the thread feeds to the needle. The tension is altered by a numbered dial or by a plus and minus indicator. There may be a second disc for sewing with two threads.

NEEDLEPLATE

The needleplate surrounds the feed dog and has a small hole for straight stitch and a slot for zigzag stitch. There may be two separate plates provided with the machine which are changed according to the type of stitching in progress, or one plate which can be turned round. The plate is held in position magnetically or by screws or clips, and has fabric guide markings.

CONTROLS ON COMPUTERIZED MACHINES

All the functions are chosen by touch control, either alone or in conjunction with dialling wheels for stitch length and width. Stop, start, reverse, stitch selection and buttonhole symbols are shown on a central selector panel.

MACHINE NEEDLES AND THREAD

NEEDLES

Modern machine needles have a rounded shank which is flattened down one side with a long groove on the opposite side. Thread the needle from the grooved side and do not use a blunt or bent needle. Needles are made in various sizes to accommodate all weights of thread, and there are different types for specific purposes. Use the correct size of needle for the fabric and change the needle frequently, especially when working with synthetics.

Basic sharp point needles are used for most general sewing purposes on woven fabrics.

Ball point needles are specially designed for sewing synthetic knitted fabric. The rounded point passes between the threads of the fabric without splitting the yarn.

Jean needles are elongated and have a very sharp point. They are strong enough to penetrate the hard texture of denim and canvas.

Leather needles have a sharpened, wedge-shaped tip to cut cleanly through leather, suede and vinyl. Never use this type of needle on fabric.

Twin and triple needles are multiple needles for pin tucks, and double or triple line stitching.

Wing needles have a wide blade which makes a hole in the fabric and they are only used for decorative stitching. A double wing needle has one wing needle and one ordinary needle fixed together.

Open needles have a slit eye to make them easy to thread.

Basting needles have two eyes, one for normal sewing and the other for machine tacking.

Perfect stitch needles have a long indentation near the eye. They are used on fine synthetic fabrics to help prevent missed stitches.

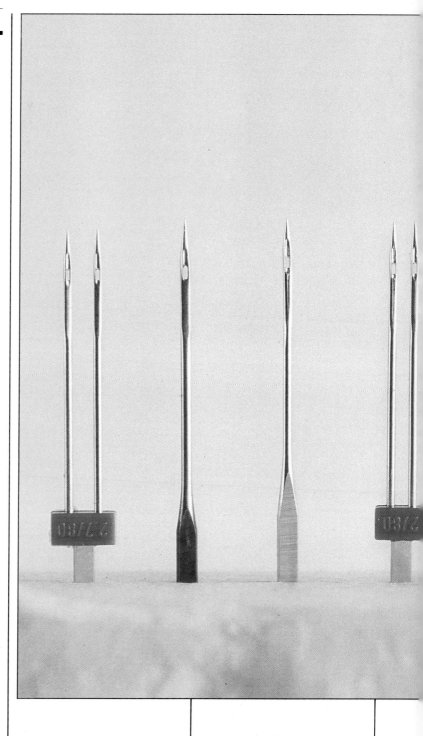

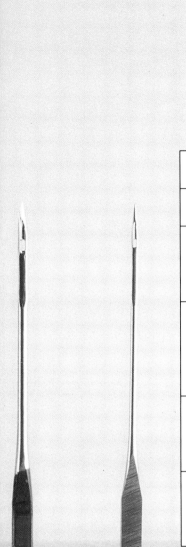

THREAD

Select a machine thread according to the type of fabric you are using. Use a polyester thread for sewing synthetics and a mercerized cotton thread for cotton and linen. Silk fabrics should always be sewn with pure silk. Wool fabrics should be sewn with a silk or synthetic thread as they will 'give' with the fabric.

NEEDLE AND THREAD SELECTION CHART

Fabric	Thread	Needle
Lightweight Chiffon, organza, fine lace, lawn, voile	Silk, mercerized cotton, extra fine (any fibre), size 60-100	70
Medium weight Velvet, gingham, crepe, brocade, linen, fine denims, polyester/cotton	Polyester, cotton-wrapped polyester, mercerized cotton, size 50-60	80
Heavy Wide rib corduroy, tweed, heavy woollens	Polyester, cotton-wrapped polyester, heavy duty (any fibre), size 30-40	90 or 100
Very heavy Canvas, upholstery fabric, heavy denim	Polyester, cotton-wrapped polyester, heavy duty (any fibre), size 20	100 or 110

Match the colour of the thread to that of the fabric, choosing one shade darker because the thread will appear lighter when stitched.

On all types of thread, the higher the number on the spool, the finer the thread. Select the number of the thread according to the weight of the fabric.

MACHINE ATTACHMENTS

All machines have special attachments for different types of stitching. Some make sewing difficult fabrics easier, some save time and some are used in conjunction with a particular needle. Your machine handbook will give details of those which are available for your machine and show you how to attach them. Some will come with your machine, while others will have to be bought separately. Attachments are usually a good investment as they will lend a more professional appearance to the items you make. A selection of machine attachments is shown below.

ZIP FOOT

A zip foot is usually supplied with most modern machines. It is also used to attach piping and is designed for stitching close to the zip teeth or the filled edge of piping. On some machines the needle position adjusts so that it will fit into the indentations on either side of the foot, on other models the zip foot is adjusted to fit to the needle. Special grooved plastic zip feet are also available for use with a concealed zip.

EMBROIDERY FOOT

An embroidery foot is made from clear plastic so that you can see what is happening underneath it. A groove is cut out underneath the foot to allow the thickness of the stitching to pass through it without becoming flattened. Use this foot for all satin stitch and decorative stitching.

BINDING FOOT

This foot applies pre-folded bias binding to raw edges. Use purchased binding or make your own from bias strips of fabric using a tape maker.

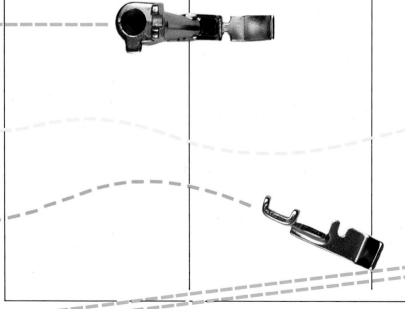

NARROW HEMMER FOOT

A hemmer foot rolls under the raw edge of the fabric to form a narrow double hem which is fed under the needle. This attachment works best with lightweight fabrics.

PIN TUCK FOOT

This foot accommodates narrow tucks in the fabric which fit into the grooves under the foot and it is used with a twin needle.

GATHERING FOOT

A gathering foot will gather a length of fabric in fixed amounts as you stitch. It can be used to gather single fabric, or to gather a frill and attach it to another piece of fabric in one operation.

TEFLON COATED FOOT

This foot is coated with Teflon in the same way as a non-stick saucepan. It is used when sewing on plastic and PVC-coated fabrics as they will pass smoothly under the foot.

ROLLER FOOT

A roller foot has two or more grooved rollers fitted into the front and back of the foot. Use it when stitching leather, plastic, velvet and slippery fabrics.

OVERLOCK FOOT

This foot is used with stitches that make a seam and neaten the raw edges of the fabric in one operation. It is a useful extra to buy if you make a lot of garments and you like this type of seam finish.

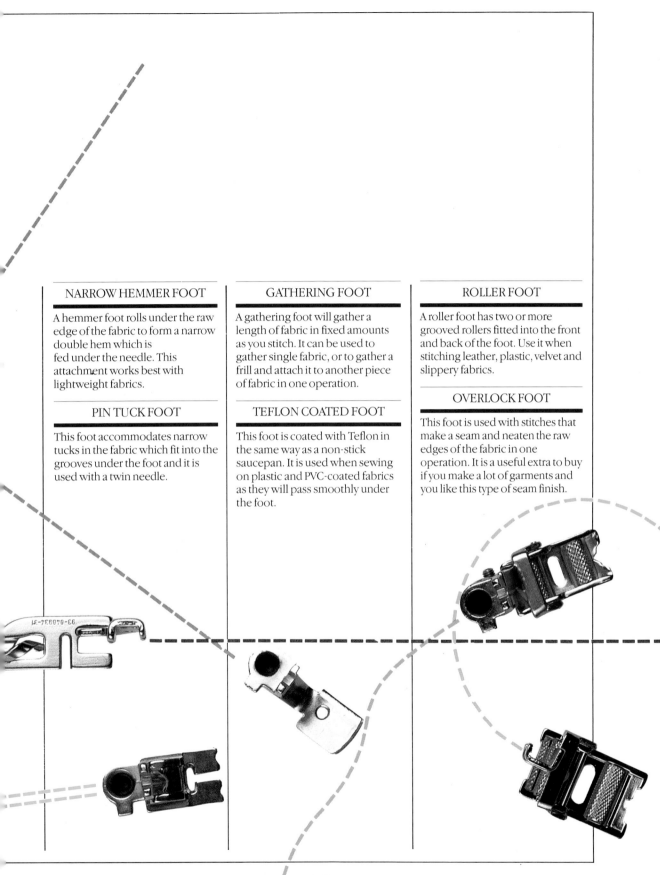

S T A R T I N G   T O   S E W

When you have bought your new sewing machine, learn to control it by practising stitching on paper and then on spare fabric. Do not thread the machine at this stage. Put a sheet of lined or squared paper under the foot, lower the foot and start to stitch along the lines. Practise stitching lines, curves and corners, reversing, changing speed and stopping and starting at marked points on the paper.

When you feel confident about your control, thread the machine according to the diagram in the handbook and practise the same techniques on a double piece of fabric. Use your hands to guide the fabric gently under the foot without pushing or pulling it. Try out all the various utility stitches and adjust the stitch length and width to see what will happen.

NEEDLE THREAD TOO LOOSE	NEEDLE THREAD CORRECT TENSION	NEEDLE THREAD TOO TIGHT
When the needle thread is too loose, it will be pulled in loops to the underneath of the fabric by the bobbin thread. This will result in too much thread for each stitch and the stitching will be loose and break easily. Correct this by lowering the foot and then turning the tension dial to a higher number or towards the plus sign.	When the two threads are tensioned correctly, the link formed between the threads is centred between the fabric layers. Equal amounts of needle and bobbin thread have been used and the stitching lies flat. A seam stitched with a balanced tension is much stronger than one stitched with an unbalanced tension.	When the tension of the needle thread is tighter than the bobbin thread, puckers will occur in the fabric along the stitched line. The bobbin thread is drawn tightly to the top of the fabric, resulting in too little thread for the stitch to be formed correctly. To correct this, lower the foot and then turn the tension dial to a lower number or towards the minus sign.

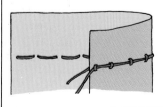

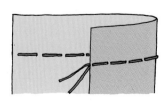

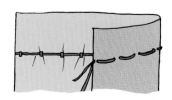

KEEPING STRAIGHT

At this point, you are ready to begin your first sewn item. Pick something simple to make and at first use just straight and zigzag stitches. Always have a guideline along which to sew: a line of tacking, a chalk line or an edge. Do not stitch directly on top of tacking, but slightly to one side towards the raw edge so that the tacking can be removed easily after the stitching is finished. Keep stitching straight by running the edge of the fabric level with the machine foot or by using the guide marked on the needleplate. Work from the wider end of the piece of fabric and stitch the seams in the same direction if possible.

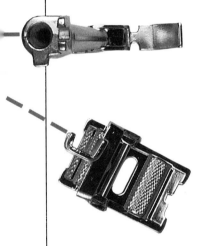

SECURING THREAD ENDS

It is important to finish the thread ends securely at each end of the stitching. Do this by reversing the direction of the stitching. Start stitching about 1cm (³⁄₈in) from the edge and reverse to the edge before stitching forwards. At the end of the line, when you are approaching the point where you want to stop, put your hand on the hand wheel to act as a brake and ease off the pressure on the foot control. All machines will stop within one or two stitches and you can use the wheel to make the final stitch by hand. Never stitch beyond the edge of the fabric. Reverse the stitching for 1cm (³⁄ ₈in) to secure the threads and cut off the surplus at each end of the stitching. When using a fine fabric fasten off the threads by hand, by running the threads through the stitching on the wrong side with a needle. On fine fabrics reverse stitching tends to pucker and should be avoided.

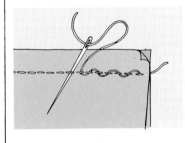

TURNING CORNERS

When you reach the corner point, turn the hand wheel so that the needle is lowered into the fabric. Raise the foot and pivot the fabric round the needle so that you can stitch along the seamline. Lower the foot and continue stitching.

On fine fabrics and those which are likely to fray, adjust the stitch to a smaller size just before turning the corner. Work a few stitches past the corner then return to the original stitch size.

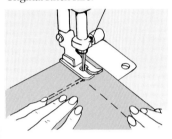

STITCHING ROUND CURVES

Stitch as normal round a gentle curve using a slow speed and easing the fabric round gradually. For a tight curve, stop stitching at the beginning of the curve and lower the needle into the fabric. Raise the foot and turn the fabric slightly in the direction of the curve. Work one or two stitches slowly and then repeat the stop, turn, stitch, sequence right round the curve. Take care to keep the stitching at an even distance from the edge of the fabric.

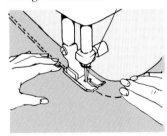

When you feel really familiar with your machine, try out the more complicated features such as buttonholes and any automatic stitch patterns. Practise them on a piece of spare fabric a few times before using them on an actual item.

GENERAL RULES FOR MACHINE STITCHING

Follow the suggestions given below to obtain a good finish to machine stitching:
● Before stitching press the fabric, using the correct iron temperature, so that it is perfectly flat and smooth.
● Use the correct size and type of needle for the fabric and the stitch.
● Change needles frequently as they soon become blunt.
● Set the stitch length and width to settings that seem suitable. Try out the stitching on a folded piece of spare fabric. Press and check both sides of the fabric to see if any

adjustments are necessary. If so, make the adjustments and test the stitching again.
● When using knitted, stretchy fabric, pull it gently to make sure the zigzag width is sufficient to prevent the stitches from snapping.
● Use the same colour and type of thread for the needle and bobbin.
● After stitching, press the line of stitches on one side of the fabric to flatten and set them into the fabric.
● Trim off any loose, fraying threads from the edges of the fabric.

Good equipment helps to give a more professional finish to your sewing. A few basic pieces of equipment are essential, so always buy the best you can afford. There is an increasing range of gadgets available which, strictly speaking, are not essential, although many of them are useful and time saving.

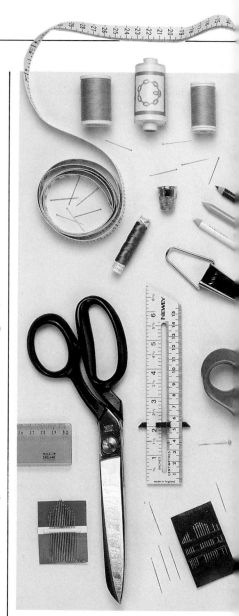

SCISSORS

Good quality scissors are a real investment as they will cut accurately and last longer than cheaper ones. Buy several pairs in different sizes and make sure they are comfortable to hold. Drop-forged scissors are quite heavy, but they can be sharpened repeatedly and, with care, they will last a lifetime. Lightweight, stainless steel scissors with plastic handles are comfortable to use and keep sharp for a long time.

Choose a large pair of scissors with 28cm (11in) blades for cutting out fabric. These should be shaped so the blade rests flat on the table while you are cutting. A medium-sized pair, 10 to 12cm (4 to 5in) long, are useful for trimming seams and cutting small pieces of fabric. A small pair will also be needed for trimming thread ends, clipping fabric edges and cutting buttonholes. Pinking shears for finishing the edges of fabric are useful, but not essential. Look after your scissors and do not cut anything other than fabric with them as they will become blunt.

BODKINS

A bodkin is used for inserting elastic or cord through a casing. It is also handy for removing tacking stitches and easing out corners and points to give a sharp finish. The elastic is tied securely round the groove at the end of the bodkin, and then inserted. An elastic threader is a flat, blunt-ended metal needle with a very large eye which is also used for threading elastic through a casing.

THIMBLES

A thimble is worn on the middle finger of the hand that holds the needle. It enables you to push the needle through the fabric painlessly, which is important if the fabric is stiff or has a very close weave.

NEEDLES

The choice of needles for hand sewing is largely a matter of personal preference. Needles are designed for specific purposes, but you may feel comfortable using a certain type.

Betweens are short needles used for most types of hand sewing, especially hemming.

Sharps are longer and used for tacking and gathering when more than one stitch is on the needle.

Straw or millinery needles are very long and are used for stitching through many layers of fabric.

Keep a range of types and sizes of needles and replace them frequently as they soon become blunt in use. Select the needle size according to the weight of fabric and thread you are using.

PINS

Buy good quality pins in a container and leave any supplied absorbent paper in with the pins as it will prevent rust. Long pins with glass or plastic heads are useful when working with openweave or hairy fabrics as they are easy to see. It is useful to keep a pincushion or magnetic pinholder by the machine.

MEASURES

Buy a fibreglass tape measure marked with metric and imperial measurements. Fabric and plastic tape measures may eventually stretch. A wooden metre ruler is essential for accurate, long measurements and for marking hems. A metal or plastic sewing gauge should also be purchased. A metal marker with a movable pointer can be used when making tucks, pleats and for marking buttonholes. A plastic set square and ruler will be needed for altering paper patterns.

TAILOR'S CHALK

Tailor's chalk is used to mark stitching lines, darts and hem lines. Use white chalk as this is the easiest to brush out after stitching. Keep the edge of the chalk sharp by paring it carefully with a blade. Chalk pencils are easy to sharpen and they have a brush at one end for removing the chalk marks from the fabric. A fabric marking pen with special ink which washes out can also be used to mark single layers of fabric.

OTHER SEWING EQUIPMENT

The following items are not essential, but they will all save time and make certain processes easier. A skirt marker will help you mark a hem line by puffing a chalk line on to the garment at a chosen height from the floor. A rouleau needle is useful for turning narrow bias tubing. A tape maker will make professional-looking bias binding from your own fabric. Battery-operated scissors are quicker but less accurate than ordinary ones. A needle threader is handy if your eyesight is less than perfect. Dressmaker's carbon paper and a tracing wheel can be used to transfer construction markings from a paper pattern to fabric. Iron-on hemming web will hold hems and facings in place. Perforated strip interfacings will make the construction of cuffs and waistbands simpler.

THREAD

Several types of thread are available for both machine and hand sewing.

Mercerized cotton thread is smooth and has a slight sheen; it comes in number 40 for general use and numbers 50 and 60 for fine fabrics and hand sewing. Use this thread for stitching cotton and linen fabrics.

Spun polyester thread is very strong and has more 'give', and should be used on stretch fabrics. It can also be used on wool fabrics.

Core-spun thread has a coating of cotton round a polyester core; it is a strong thread, slightly thicker than polyester. Use it on all types of fabric except fine ones.

Pure silk thread is strong and lustrous and very good for hand sewing. Use silk thread on silk and wool fabrics.

Tacking thread breaks easily so it can be removed without damaging the fabric. Never use tacking thread for any other purpose because it is not strong enough.

Thicker thread called button-hole twist is made from polyester or silk and used for top stitching, working hand-stitched button-holes and sewing on buttons.

PRESSING EQUIPMENT

Pressing is a very important part of sewing. Each seam and dart should be pressed as soon as it is stitched to give it a clean, crisp finish. Your pressing equipment should always be ready to use when you are sewing.

THE IRON

The ideal iron for home-sewing purposes should be fairly heavy and capable of both dry and steam pressing. It should have a wide range of temperatures so that you can select the correct one for the fabric type. A spray for dampening stubborn creases is a useful extra feature.

THE IRONING BOARD

A sturdy, well made ironing board is essential. It should be adjustable so that it is a comfortable height for you to work at, and it should have a well padded cover, which does not wrinkle. Add an extra layer of padding under the cover if it seems rather thin and flat.

TAILOR'S HAM

This is a firmly padded cushion with rounded ends which is used when pressing curved areas such as darts and curved seams. A pressing mitt serves the same function, but it is smaller and can be slipped over your hand or the tip of a sleeve board.

PRESSING CLOTHS

Have a selection of clean white cloths for pressing. Use cheese-cloth for pressing lightweight fabrics and cotton or linen for heavier weights. Discard a pressing cloth as soon as it becomes discoloured or scorched.

SLEEVE BOARD

A sleeve board looks like a miniature ironing board and is used on top of the normal board. It is designed for pressing narrow areas that will not thread on to an ironing board, so you are able to press a single layer of fabric at a time. A seam roll is a tightly packed cylindrical cushion that is used for pressing seams in the same restricted areas.

OPTIONAL EQUIPMENT

Other pressing aids are available which are useful if you intend to make tailored garments or work with heavy fabrics.

A wooden tailor's board has curves and straight edges and is used for precision pressing. A point presser is similar and is used for pressing corners and points. A tailor's clapper is a heavy block of wood used to pound creases into heavy fabric after it has been steamed. Press pile fabrics over a needleboard that has a flat surface covered with steel wires, which will prevent the pile being flattened when it is pressed. A pressing pad is composed of layers of soft fabric stitched together and it is used to press raised areas such as embroidered monograms so that they are not flattened.

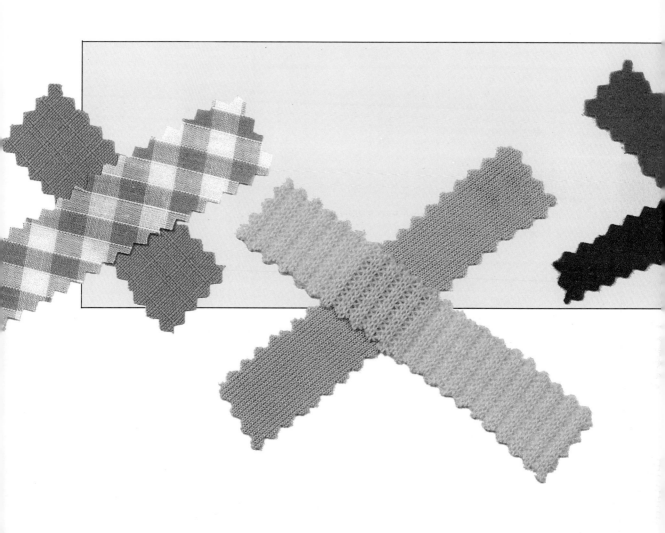

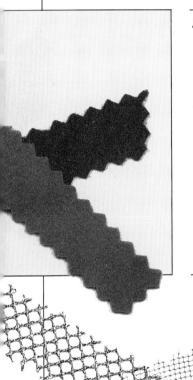

Successful sewing depends to a great extent on the right choice of fabrics. This chapter provides a directory of the numerous fabrics available, giving details of how they are made, and what they are most suitable for. It suggests guidelines on judging the performance of different kinds of material and on how best to care for your fabrics.

FABRIC TYPES

Fabrics are made from different types of fibres which can be used singly or in combinations of two, three or more. These fibres may be natural, such as wool, linen, cotton and silk, or man-made, such as acrylic, polyester and acetate. With the exception of silk, all natural fibres are short and are called staples. Silk and some man-made synthetic fibres take the form of long, continuous strands called filaments. The staples and filament lengths are twisted into yarns which are then made into a fabric. The appearance and durability of the yarn is affected by the degree of twist, with tightly twisted yarns being in general the smoothest and strongest.

Fabric is formed using one of a variety of techniques: weaving, knitting, felting or netting.

WEAVING

This is the most usual method of making fabric, in which two sets of yarns (the warp and the weft) are woven together to produce a fabric. The warp threads run lengthwise down the fabric and they are crossed at right angles by the weft threads. The weave can be either plain or patterned according to the arrangement of the threads.

KNITTING

Knitted fabric is stretchy and comfortable to wear. The fabric is formed by a series of interlocking loops. Weft-knitted fabric has the loops running crosswise and the stretch is greater across the fabric than down it. Warp-knitted fabric is made by forming the loops lengthwise and is more stable and durable than the weft-knitted type.

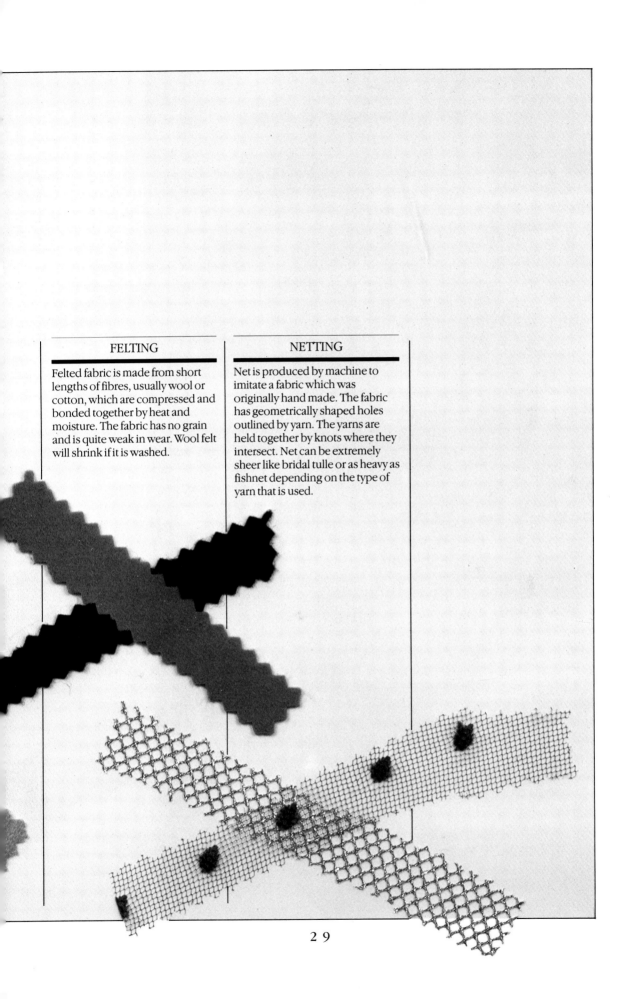

FELTING

Felted fabric is made from short lengths of fibres, usually wool or cotton, which are compressed and bonded together by heat and moisture. The fabric has no grain and is quite weak in wear. Wool felt will shrink if it is washed.

NETTING

Net is produced by machine to imitate a fabric which was originally hand made. The fabric has geometrically shaped holes outlined by yarn. The yarns are held together by knots where they intersect. Net can be extremely sheer like bridal tulle or as heavy as fishnet depending on the type of yarn that is used.

FABRIC CHOICE

COTTON AND LINEN

WOOL AND SILK

COTTON AND LINEN

Cotton is made from the fibres of the cotton plant. Plants grown in different areas of the world produce varying lengths and weights of fibre. The best quality cotton fabric is made with yarn spun from long, fine fibres such as Sea Island and Egyptian cotton. Cotton fabric is hard wearing, strong and absorbent, which makes it ideal for garments and home furnishings. Cotton does, however, crease in use and can shrink when it is washed. These problems can be overcome by special finishes or by the addition of a small amount of synthetic fibres.

Linen is made from the fibres which come from the stem of the flax plant. It is one of the oldest fibres in existence and, although expensive, it is extremely strong and hard wearing. Cotton is often added to linen for economy reasons and this mixture is an excellent fabric for heavy, winter curtains and upholstery. Fabric made from linen is inclined to crease badly during use and the addition of synthetic fibres can prevent this.

Batiste A soft, sheer, lightweight fabric named after the French weaver, Jean Batiste. Cotton, linen, or a mix of the two, batiste may be used for summer dresses and shirts, infant wear and lingerie.

Brocade A fabric with areas of different weaves which create a raised pattern. Brocade can be cotton, synthetic, silk, or a blend.

Broderie Anglaise A decorative embroidered fabric in which holes are cut or punched into a base fabric and the open areas surrounded by embroidery stitches. Originally hand stitched, Broderie Anglaise is now made by machine. It is often used in narrow strips for edging garments. Although many different fabrics can be used as a base for the embroidery, white cotton or cotton blends are probably most common.

Calico A lightweight, plain-weave cotton or cotton-blended fabric often printed with small floral patterns or other effects. Plain, unbleached calico is also used in home furnishings. Calico originated in Calcutta, India.

Cambric A plain-weave fabric that is finished with a slightly glossy surface. Traditionally cambric is made from cotton or linen but it can also be made from synthetics.

Canvas This term applies to several different fabrics, including cotton, linen and synthetics. Canvas with a heavy, close weave is used for upholstery, making sails, awnings, tents and for industrial purposes. The stiff open-weave mesh used for needlework is also called canvas. This term includes a linen fabric used as an interfacing in hand tailoring.

Chambray A cotton or cotton blend fabric in which the warp yarns are coloured and the weft yarns are white. Chambray variations can include checks, stripes and small figured or dobby designs.

Chintz A glazed, medium-weight cotton fabric used for home furnishings. Chintz is traditionally printed with a pattern of flowers and birds.

Corduroy A corded fabric in which the rib has been sheared after it is woven to produce a smooth, velvet-like nap. Traditionally made of cotton, corduroy can also be made from a cotton and synthetic blend which is crease resistant.

Damask Similar to brocade, damask has a flatter finish with a pattern produced by the contrast of areas of satin weave against a plain background. It is a popular fabric for tablecloths and napkins and can be made from cotton or linen.

Denim A twill-weave fabric usually made of cotton or cotton blend in which, traditionally, the warp yarns were dyed blue and the weft yarns were white.

Drill A sturdy, durable, twill-weave fabric of medium-weight. Usually made of cotton or cotton blends, drill is used for garments and home furnishings.

Gauze A sheer, lightweight fabric with a fairly open weave. In recent years handwoven cotton and cotton blend gauzes from India have been popular for both summer garments and curtains.

Gingham A firm lightweight fabric made from cotton or cotton and polyester, with a woven pattern of regular checks.

Lace An open-work patterned fabric made either on a background fabric of net or without a background fabric. Lace can be made from cotton, nylon, viscose, silk or blends and the patterns are usually floral in design. Modern lace is nearly always made by machine and many traditional hand-made lace patterns are copied. Lace is the traditional bridal fabric but is also used for other garments and for home furnishings. Different types of lace include Brussels, Guipure, Nottingham and Chantilly.

Lawn A fairly sheer, lightweight fabric made originally from linen but now usually made from combed cotton or blends of cotton and polyester. It can be plain, printed or have woven stripes.

Linen union A heavy blend of cotton and linen used for upholstery and heavy curtains.

Madras A hand-woven cotton fabric that originated in Madras, India. It is dyed in brilliant colours and often has a woven pattern of plaids, stripes or checks. The dyes fade during washing to give the patterns a pleasantly muted colouring.

Muslin A plain-weave fabric usually woven from cotton or cotton blends. Muslin is made in a variety of weights, ranging from a sheer quality for light garments to a heavier fabric suitable for bed-linen.

Organdie Originally, organdie was a sheer cotton fabric with a stiff finish and organza was the same fabric made of silk. These distinctions have now almost disappeared and the two names are sometimes synonymous. Organdie is also made from synthetics and blends of cotton and synthetic.

Piqué A fabric woven with small, raised ribs or geometric patterns which is usually made from cotton or a blend of cotton and polyester. It is a crisp fabric that can be printed with colourful designs. White piqué is the classic fabric for tennis clothes and detachable collars and cuffs.

Plissé A puckered effect produced on cotton fabrics by shrinking some areas of the fabric with a chemical, caustic soda. The finish is reasonably permanent, but plissé fabrics should not be ironed as the puckers will become flattened.

Poplin A light to medium-weight cotton with fine cross ribs formed by using a weft yarn which is thicker than the warp.

Sateen A strong, satin-weave fabric made of cotton which can be plain or printed.

Seersucker A crinkled fabric made from cotton, cotton blends, or nylon. The crinkles are permanent and are not lost during laundering and wear.

Terry cloth An absorbent fabric made of cotton or blends of cotton and other fibres. It has uncut loops on one or both sides and is noted for its ability to absorb moisture. Terry cloth is used primarily for towels, but it is also used for garments.

Voile A light, delicate cotton or silk fabric used for summer garments and lightweight curtains.

FABRIC DIRECTORY

WOOL AND SILK

Wool fabrics are made from yarn spun from the fleece of sheep. It is hard wearing, soft and absorbent and has good insulating properties. Wool yarns come in two distinct types: woollen and worsted. Woollen yarns are generally made from shorter fibres. Worsted yarns are smoother and are made from longer fibres. Other types of wool fabrics are made from the coats of goats, rabbits and camels.

Silk is an ancient and expensive natural fibre produced from the cocoon of the silkworm. It is soft and extremely strong as well as having an attractive appearance.

Alpaca A South American goat-like animal gives its name to the wool that comes from its fleece. Fabric woven from alpaca fibres is soft, warm and silky. Alpaca fibres can be blended with cotton, wool or viscose.

Angora Long, silky fibres from the coat of the angora rabbit, which are blended with wool or synthetics to make a soft, fluffy fabric.

Barathea A fine, closely woven, smooth wool fabric with a broken rib pattern.

Bouclé A rough, looped wool fabric with a textured, knobbled surface that is usually dull unless a shiny synthetic fibre is added.

Camel hair A fibre which is obtained from the underhair of the Bactrian camel. The fibre is light brown in colour and because the colour cannot be removed easily, camel hair fabrics are generally found in natural or dark colours. The fabric is lustrous, soft, but not very hard wearing. Camel hair is often blended with sheep's wool to add durability.

Cashmere A soft, luxurious fibre from the underhair of the cashmere goat, which is made into an attractive fabric. Cashmere fabric is not hard wearing.

Challis A soft, lightweight, plain-weave fabric originally made of worsted wool but now also made from synthetic fibres. Challis is frequently printed in small floral or paisley patterns.

Crepe A fabric with a nubby, crinkly surface made from wool, silk or synthetic fibres.

Flannel A plain or twill-weave fabric of medium-weight with a napped finish, usually made of wool or cotton.

Foulard A lightweight fabric in a plain or twill weave, originally made from silk, now also made from synthetics. Foulard is often printed with small patterns on solid colour backgrounds.

Gaberdine A wool or cotton fabric which has a close, firm, twill weave.

Harris tweed A woollen tweed which is handwoven from yarns spun on the islands of the Outer Hebrides off the coast of Scotland. The yarns may be spun by hand or machine.

Herringbone A twill-weave woollen fabric in which the warp and weft yarns interlace to produce a pattern resembling the backbone of the herring fish.

Honan A type of silk fabric woven from wild silk, originally made in the Honan region of China. Wild silk is more uneven and coarse than cultivated silk and the fabric has an interesting texture.

Irish Tweed A woollen tweed that is usually made with a white warp and coloured weft.

Llama Hair from the fleece of this South American animal is often used alone or blended with wool to make a fine and lustrous fabric. The natural colours of llama hair are predominantly black or brown.

Mohair Fibre from the angora goat which is lustrous, smooth and hard wearing. Mohair fibre is often blended with wool and other fibres and the fabric is used to make garments and home furnishings.

Pongee A light or medium-weight silk fabric made from wild silk which is available in a wide range of colours.

Satin One of the basic weaves of silk fabrics. Silk satin is expensive so the fabric is now imitated by various synthetic fibres. Types of fabrics include antique, double faced, duchesse and slipper satin.

Serge A durable fabric with a close, twill weave. At one time serge was always made of worsted wool, but now is made in a variety of synthetic fibres as well.

Shantung A fabric originally made from silk, but now also in cotton and synthetic fibres. The yarn is slubbed and irregular giving a nubby texture.

Spun silk A medium-weight inexpensive matt silk. The yarn from which spun silk is woven is made from short, waste lengths of silk filament.

Tartan A pattern made of intersecting stripes. Each tartan pattern is associated with a specific family or area group, called a clan. Tartan fabrics are usually made from wool and occasionally from cotton.

Thai silk An iridescent silk fabric made in Thailand which is often slubbed and dyed in vivid colours.

Tussah A heavy, wild silk fabric with an attractive, uneven weave.

Tweed A hard wearing, woven fabric characterized by coloured slubs of yarn on a hairy surface. Tweed may be made of any fibre combination, although wool tweed is probably the most common.

Vicuna A fibre from the coat of the vicuna, a wild animal that lives in the Andes mountains. Although some vicuna have been domesticated, the animal is found mostly in the wild and must be killed to obtain the hair which is one of the softest, finest fibres known; the hair is spun and woven into an expensive fabric. The fibres are difficult to dye, and the fabric is usually found in the natural colour, a light tan to chestnut brown.

Wild silk The silk from uncultivated silkworms which is rougher and more uneven than cultivated silk. The fabric is usually duller in finish and rougher in texture than other types of silk.

Woollen A fabric made from wool fibres which have been carded before they are spun. A woollen fabric is rough, hairy and fairly hard wearing.

Worsted A type of wool fabric or yarn. Worsted fabrics are made from yarns that have been combed as well as carded. Worsted yarns are smoother than woollen yarns and make a hard-wearing fabric with a clean, smooth surface as opposed to the hairy surface of woollens.

FABRIC DIRECTORY

MAN-MADE FIBRES

Man-made fibres are the twentieth-century addition to the range of natural fibres used to make yarns and fabrics.

These fibres include those made from a natural substance, such as acetate, as well as synthetics made from chemicals. Synthetics are cheap to produce and have easy care properties unlike many of the natural fibres which crease and shrink badly and need careful laundering. However, they are less comfortable to wear and most of them lack the distinctive appearance of wool, silk, linen and cotton. Many modern fabrics are made from blends of natural and synthetic fibres to give the best of both worlds.

Acetate Acetate is a cellulose-based fibre which has been available since 1918. It is made from dissolved cotton fibres or wood shavings. The result is extruded to form a yarn which is soft, silky and moth and mildew resistant. Acetate is used to make imitation silk fabrics and is also blended with silk and cotton.

Acrylic Acrylic yarns have been available since the early 1950s and they are warmer than the other synthetics such as nylon and polyester. Acrylic fabrics are often an imitation of wool fabrics, and they are light, soft and crease resistant. Dralon is a trade name for an acrylic fibre often used for furnishing fabrics such as Dralon velvet.

Modacrylic A modified version of acrylic fibres which is almost completely flame resistant.

Modal Modal is a cellulose-based fibre which is very similar to cotton, but more absorbent. It is often blended with cotton or polyester to produce an inexpensive, comfortable fabric suitable for garments.

Polyamide This fibre is also known as nylon and it has been available since 1938. Either a filament or staple yarn, it is strong, lightweight, washes well and dries quickly. Polyamide yarns do not crease and they are resistant to moth and mildew. The fibres mix well with others and they are used in a variety of fabrics.

Polyester Polyester is a versatile fibre that can be spun and woven to imitate silk, cotton, wool or linen. It is crease resistant, easy care and hard wearing, and it is often blended with cotton to add these properties to a fabric.

PVC (polyvinyl chloride) PVC is a waterproof, synthetic plastic which is usually fused to a knitted or woven cotton backing. It comes in various weights and can be plain or printed.

Triacetate Triacetate is a modified version of acetate with similar properties, but with a more lustrous appearance.

Viscose rayon Viscose rayon was the first man-made fibre to be produced on a large scale and it has been available since 1910. It is cellulose based and is now usually blended with other fibres as it does not wear well when used alone.

Special fabrics include velvets, fur and fur fabric, knits and leather.

Astrakhan cloth A heavy woven or knitted fabric with a curly pile which imitates the natural fur, Persian lamb.

Candlewick A thick, soft yarn used to form tufts by pulling it through a base fabric and then cutting it. The term also describes the fabric made with this yarn that is used to make bedspreads and cushions.

Double cloth Reversible fabrics made with three to five sets of yarns. Some doublecloth fabrics appear the same on both sides, some have a reversed pattern, and others are different on each side, depending on the techniques used for weaving the fabric.

Double knit A knitted fabric which has one knit stitch directly behind another, so that the fabric is the same on both sides.

Fake fur A fabric which imitates animal pelts. The most popular fake furs are made from modacrylic fibre.

Felt A non-woven wool fabric made from fibres that have been joined through the natural felting qualities of the fibre. Wool and some other animal hair fibres felt naturally when subjected to the application of heat, moisture and pressure. Felt is mainly used as a decoration as it is weak and tears easily.

Flocked fabric A fabric to which short fibres have been attached with an adhesive. Flocked fabrics can be made to simulate materials such as suede and velvet. The fibres can be applied over all the fabric surface or in selected areas to form patterns.

Fur Fur is the coat of an animal which is used in the same ways as fabric. Types of fur include rabbit, mink, fox, sable, sheepskin and chinchilla.

Fusible fabric A fabric which can be joined to another fabric in a fairly permanent bond through the application of heat, moisture and pressure.

Interfacing A layer of fabric placed under the main fabric to support and strengthen it. Interfacing can be either sewn in or fused to the main fabric.

Interlining An extra layer of fabric in a garment that is intended to provide additional warmth or support a loosely woven fabric.

Jacquard knit A knitted fabric with the design knitted into the fabric in a regular all-over pattern.

Lamé A fabric woven or knitted with all metallic yarns or with a combination of metallic and other fibre yarns.

Leather The hide of an animal with the fur removed or the skin of a reptile. Leather has been used throughout history for clothing and other purposes. Today, synthetic fabrics which imitate leather are widely available. Common leather names include alligator, buckskin, calfskin, chamois, cowhide, crocodile, kid, lambskin, morocco, nappa, patent, peccary, pigskin, skiver, snakeskin and suede.

Lining A layer of fabric that gives a neat finish to the inside of an article. Lining fabrics are made from inexpensive types of silk or man-made fibres.

Net A fabric which is constructed by knotting and looping a continuous yarn to form an open mesh.

Pattern knit A knitted fabric made by dropping, adding, rearranging and crossing various stitches to create intricate designs.

Plain or single knit A flat-surfaced knitted fabric with a smooth face and looped reverse.

Raschel knit A knitted fabric which imitates crochet or net.

Rib knit A knitted fabric which consists of groups of alternate plain and purl stitches.

Tulle A very fine net made originally from silk and now made from nylon.

Velvet A fabric with a short, closely woven pile made from silk, cotton and synthetics. There are two method of making velvet. One methods uses a double cloth construction in which two layers of fabric are woven with long threads joining them. After weaving, the joining threads are cut, producing two pieces of velvet. In the other weaving process, the yarn is lifted over wires to form the pile. When the wires are removed, the yarn is cut to form the pile.

Wadding Wadding is a thick layer of compressed polyester or cotton fibres that is used in quilting.

FABRIC FINISHES

FABRIC FINISHES

The handle and performance of a fabric can be changed by the addition of a special finish. Check the label on the fabric you buy to see if it has a finish and whether there are any special fabric care instructions. The most common fabric finishes are described below.

Colourfast The dyes used on the fabric will not run during washing provided that the fabric care instructions are followed. This finish will also prevent colours from fading in direct sunlight.

Crease resistant The fabric has been treated so that it will shed creases. This finish does not mean that creasing will be totally prevented.

Flame resistant The fabric has been treated so that it will not burn once the source of the fire has been removed. This is especially important when choosing fabric for making nightwear and children's clothes.

Mercerized This finish is found on cotton fabrics and sewing threads. It strengthens the fibres and gives them a slight sheen.

Mothproof This finish is found on wool and silk fabrics that are prone to damage by moth larvae.

Pre-shrunk The fabric has been shrunk during manufacture and will not shrink more than one or two per cent during laundering.

Stain repellent This finish is found mainly on furnishing fabrics and means that the fabric has been treated to resist staining.

Wash and wear The fabric has been treated so that it can be washed and worn without requiring ironing. Repeated washing will eventually destroy the finish.

Water repellent This finish reduces the water absorption of fibres and is found on cotton and nylon fabrics. An alternative name for this finish is 'showerproof'. This finish does not mean that the fabric is totally waterproof.

CHOOSING FABRICS

Successful sewing depends to a great extent on the right choice of fabrics. The colour and pattern of the fabric is, of course, largely a matter of personal preference and the amount of money available, but the following points should also be taken into consideration.

When choosing fabric for a garment, stand in front of a mirror and drape the fabric in front of you. Check that it will suit your colouring and that the weight of the fabric is suitable for the style of garment that you have in mind.

When choosing fabric to make up into an item for the home, take colour samples of your existing fabrics, wallpaper and paint to check that the colour match or contrast will work well.

Crush a corner of the fabric in your hand and see whether it will spring back into shape without creasing badly.

Check the raw edges of the fabric for excessive fraying. If your chosen fabric does fray badly, allow 5mm ($\frac{1}{4}$in) extra on the seam allowances when cutting out.

Pull knit fabrics gently lengthwise and widthwise to check the 'give'. Make sure that the fabric springs back into its original shape after stretching.

Look at the pattern or weave to see if the fabric has a 'one way' pattern or a nap. You may need to buy extra fabric if this is the case.

Check the straightness of the grain.

Unroll some of the metreage (yardage) of the fabric and check if there are any flaws.

Check the fibre composition of the fabric and whether there are any special finishes and cleaning instructions.

AFTER - CARE OF FABRICS

Launder fabric items carefully to make sure that they last as long as possible. Follow any instructions given when the fabric was purchased and dry clean if the washability is in doubt. Clean fabric items before they become really dirty otherwise the dirt may become ingrained and difficult to remove. This is especially important for white and pastel coloured fabrics, and synthetics which tend to hold the dirt.

INTERNATIONAL CARE SYMBOLS

Standardized washing information is now given in the form of a series of international symbols. The five main symbols for washing, bleaching, dry cleaning, ironing and drying are shown below. A cross through any of these symbols means 'do not use'
① This symbol represents the washing process and all instructions relating to it.
② The triangle represents chlorine bleaching instructions.
③ The iron represents ironing instructions including temperatures, which are indicated by dots inside the symbol. One dot indicates the temperature for man-made fabrics, two dots are for polyester blends, silk and wool, and three dots are for cotton, linen and viscose.
④ The circle represents dry cleaning and the type of solvent which should be used.
⑤ This symbol represents tumble drying which may be either harmful or beneficial for some fabrics.

WASHING SYMBOLS

These symbols are also found on packs of washing powder and they give a reliable temperature guide.

① White cotton and linen articles without special finishes.

② Cotton, linen or viscose articles. No special finishes: colours fast at 60°C (140°F).

③ White nylon, white polyester and cotton blends.

④ Coloured nylon, cotton and viscose blends with special finishes, coloured polyester/cotton blends.

⑤ Cotton, linen and viscose articles where colours are fast at 40°C (104°F), but not at 60°C (140°F).

⑥ Acrylic, acetate and triacetate, including blends with wool, polyester and wool blends.

⑦ Wool, wool blends with cotton or viscose, silk.

⑧ Silk and printed acetate fabrics with colours not fast at 40°C (104°F).

⑨ Cotton articles with special finishes which can be boiled but require drip drying.

⑩ Hand wash only.

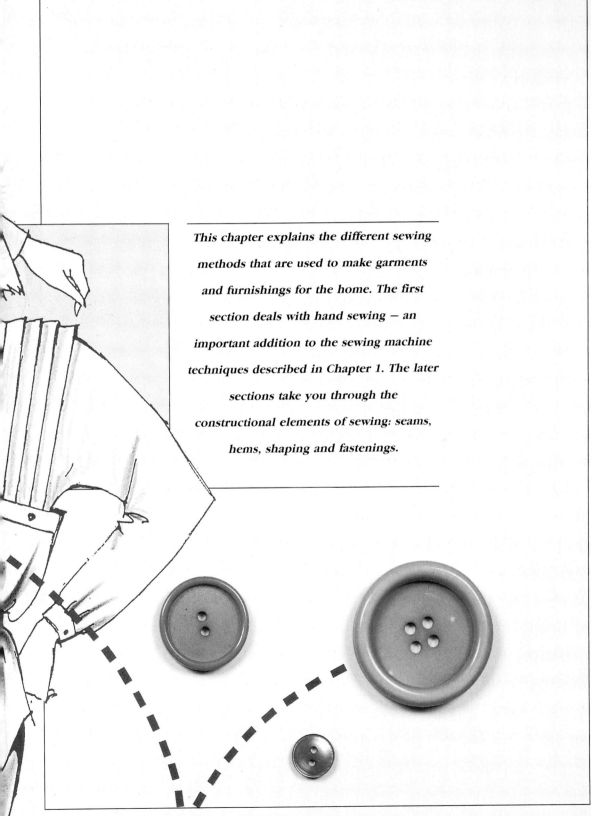

This chapter explains the different sewing methods that are used to make garments and furnishings for the home. The first section deals with hand sewing – an important addition to the sewing machine techniques described in Chapter 1. The later sections take you through the constructional elements of sewing: seams, hems, shaping and fastenings.

H A N D   S E W I N G

Most garments and items for the home are made initially on the machine and then finished by hand. Hand finishing should be neat and unobtrusive, so take care to use the correct stitch for the job in hand otherwise the results could be disappointing. If you are not familiar with some of the stitches shown, take time to practise them on a piece of spare fabric until you feel confident with your technique. Never try to hurry hand sewing – it should be an enjoyable and relaxed process. The size of needle to use when sewing by hand is largely a matter of personal preference, but a fine needle will generally give a neater result.

STARTING TO SEW

Good light is essential when sewing. Sit in a comfortable chair where there is good natural light, or use a directional lamp. Assemble the equipment you will need before you begin sewing and keep it together within easy reach. Make sure that your hands are scrupulously clean and try to use a thimble to prevent wear and tear on the fingers. When sewing white fabrics, a shake of talcum powder on your hands will help to prevent the fabric becoming fingermarked.

Use a small knot at the end of the thread unless you are working on a fine, delicate fabric, when a few tiny stitches should be used to secure the end. Hide the knot under a fold or at the edge of the fabric if the stitching is to be permanent. Keep the length of working thread fairly short to prevent it from tangling. Fasten off the thread with two or three back stitches, again hiding them under a fold or at the edge of the fabric.

Keeping the correct tension when hand sewing is just as important as when you are using a machine. It should be correct for the fabric – if it is too tight, puckers and wrinkles will occur. When stitching is loose, the layers of fabric will part and the stitching could eventually break. The secret of even tension is practice and familiarity with the particular stitch you are using.

TACKING STITCH OR BASTING

Tacking is used to keep layers of fabric together temporarily after pinning and before machine stitching. Use a thread that contrasts well with the fabric to make the tacking easy to remove. The stitches should be between 5mm (¼in) and 1cm (⅜in) long.

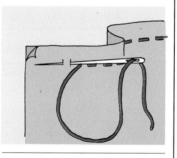

UNEVEN TACKING STITCH

Uneven tacking is also used to hold layers of fabric together, but although it is quicker, it is not as strong as the previous stitch. Take long stitches on one side of the fabric and short stitches on the reverse.

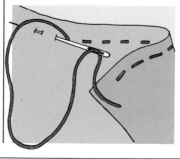

DIAGONAL TACKING STITCH

Diagonal tacking is used to hold layers of fabric firmly together within an area. It keeps the fabric flat where a row of ordinary tacking could cause a ridge; for example, when attaching interfacing or holding a pleat in place. Take horizontal stitches from right to left through the fabric as shown to leave a row of diagonal stitches on the right side.

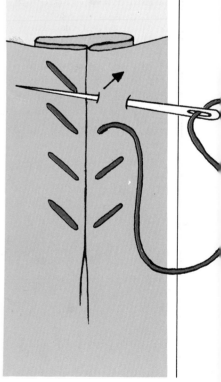

RUNNING STITCH

Running stitch is used mainly for gathering and shirring fabric. It looks like a smaller version of tacking stitch, but it is worked differently. Take several small stitches on to the point of the needle before pulling it through the fabric. When gathering fabric, make sure that the thread is long enough to make an unbroken line of stitching.

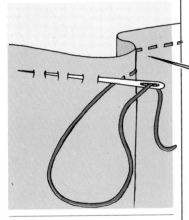

HALF BACK STITCH

Half back stitch is similar to ordinary back stitch but a longer stitch is taken on the reverse of the fabric which spaces out the stitches on the front. From the front, the stitches should form a neat, broken line. When the stitches on the front are very tiny, this stitch is known as prick stitch.

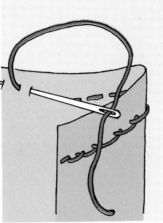

OVERSEWING

Oversewing is used instead of slip stitch to join two folded edges of fabric when a strong join is needed. Work from right to left as shown taking a small amount of fabric from each fold. Pull the sewing thread quite tightly to give a neat join.

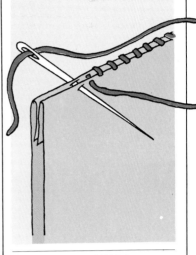

BACK STITCH

Back stitch is a strong stitch which can be used to make a garment if a machine is not available. It is also used to stitch parts of a garment which are awkward to reach with a machine. The stitches on the front of the work look like machine stitches, and they should be small and worked perfectly evenly. Two or three back stitches worked on top of each other can also be used to finish hand stitching.

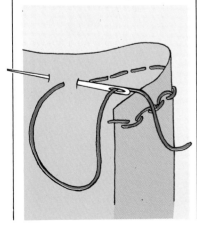

OVERCASTING

Overcasting is used to neaten the edges of fabrics which fray easily. Work from either direction, taking the thread over the edge of the fabric. Do not pull the thread too tightly as the edges of the fabric will curl and make bulges. If the fabric frays badly, work a row of machine stitching first and trim the fabric close to this stitching before overcasting over the edge and the machine stitching.

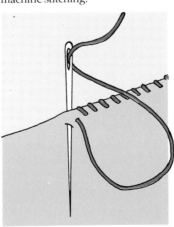

STAB STITCH

Stab stitch is a small, strong stitch worked through several layers of fabric. It is a good stitch to use when attaching a zip by hand as it is almost invisible on the right side. Stab stitch looks similar to half back stitch, but it is worked with a stabbing motion through the fabric layers. Work stab stitch from the right side as it is untidy on the reverse.

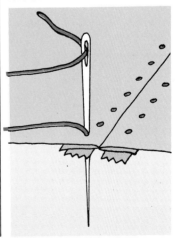

BLANKET STITCH

Blanket stitch is a looped stitch mainly used for neatening raw edges. The loops can be close together or spaced apart, depending on where the stitch is used. Open blanket stitch, with the stitches set widely apart, is also used as an alternative to herringbone stitch for finishing edges and holding them down. Close blanket stitch is used over bar tacks and button shanks.

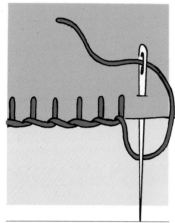

HEM STITCH

Hem stitch is used to hold down the fold of a hem on light and medium-weight fabrics. This stitch may show on the right side and the thread should not be pulled taut as the fabric may pucker. Work as shown, picking up a thread of the single fabric and then a thread of the fold before pulling the needle through.

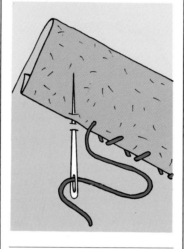

SLIP STITCH

Slip stitch is used to join two folded edges of fabric and, if worked carefully, should be almost invisible. It can be worked from the right side which makes it especially useful for finishing the ends of ties, waistbands and cuffs. Pull the thread sufficiently to join the folds securely, but take care as the fabric will wrinkle if the tension is too tight. Slip stitch is also used to finish hems on fine, delicate fabrics.

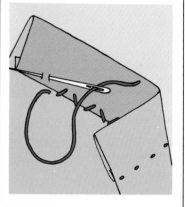

TAILOR'S BUTTONHOLE STITCH

This stitch is used for working buttonholes in preference to close blanket stitch as it is stronger and more hard wearing. Worked in a similar way, it forms a row of knots against the raw edge. Always keep the stitches close together and make sure that the knots touch in order to keep the edge firm.

BLIND HEM STITCH

Blind hem stitch is worked on the inside fold of a hem and worked from right to left. The stitches are almost invisible, providing the thread is not pulled tightly, making it ideal for skirt or dress hems. This stitch can also be used to hold down a fold of fabric which has had the raw edge neatened by hand overcasting or by a machine zigzag stitch.

HERRINGBONE STITCH

Although primarily an embroidery stitch, herringbone stitch is used in hand sewing for securing hems on heavy fabrics. Work it directly over the raw edge, and the edge will be neatened at the same time. Herringbone stitch is fairly elastic so it is ideal for use with stretch fabrics and knits.

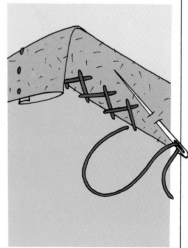

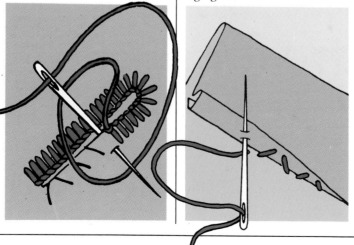

TAILOR'S TACKS

Tailor's tacks are the most accurate method of transferring markings from a paper pattern to double layers of fabric. Use them to mark seamlines, darts, and other construction symbols and also to mark delicate fabrics, which may be damaged by using other methods such as a tracing wheel. Always leave the pattern pinned to the fabric until all marks have been transferred from it. With the point of the needle, slit the pattern across the symbol to be marked before working the tailor's tack and always use double thread. Take care not to pull the tacks out when lifting the pattern off the fabric. After the pattern has been removed, gently separate the layers of fabric and cut the loops with sharp scissors.

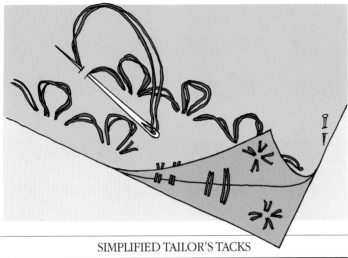

FELL STITCH

Fell stitch is also known as felling, and it is used in tailoring to attach loose linings to the neckline, seams and front edges of coats and jackets. Tack the lining in position with the raw edge folded under, and work with this fold away from you as shown. The stitches should be neat, tiny and almost invisible. The join made will be extremely strong.

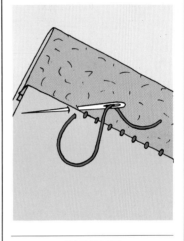

SIMPLIFIED TAILOR'S TACKS

Simplified tailor's tacks are used to mark a line of pleats or a seamline on a single piece of fabric. They consist of a continuous row of loose stitches in double thread as shown. Cut the thread between each stitch before removing the pattern carefully, taking care not to pull out the markings.

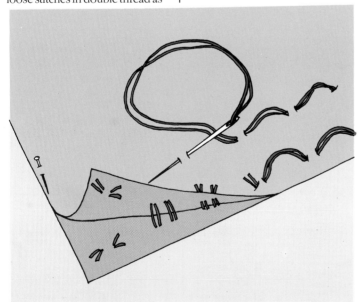

BAR TACK

A bar tack is a strengthening device used to prevent fabric tearing, for example, at the base of a zip or across the end of a sleeve opening. A bar of straight stitches is worked through the fabric first. Closely spaced blanket stitches are then worked over this bar without the needle penetrating the fabric. Take care to fasten off the thread securely on the wrong side of the fabric.

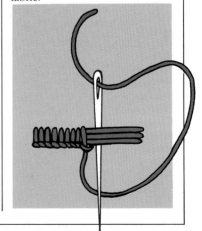

P L A I N   S E A M S

Seams are formed when two or more pieces of fabric are joined together by a line of stitching. They are the main constructional element in sewing, and should be worked with care. Seams are usually machine stitched, but they can be sewn by hand using back stitch.

Plain seams create the shape of a garment or item of home furnishing and should be almost invisible when pressed. Decorative seams emphasize the lines of shaping and are often used as a strong design feature. The choice of seam will also depend on the weight of the fabric and the type of article being made. For example, a run and fell seam used on denim jeans will be more durable and suitable for repeated laundering than a flat seam.

FLAT SEAM

A flat seam is the basic method used to join fabrics of normal weight. It is always sewn with the right sides of the fabric facing, and the raw edges should be finished to prevent fraying. Neaten straight flat seams after stitching and pressing open. A plain straight stitch should be used on woven fabric with the appropriate sizes of needle and thread.

Stretch fabric needs to be sewn with a stitch which allows the seam to 'give', otherwise the stitching will break during use. A small straight stitch and polyester thread will often give sufficient stretch or a very narrow machine zigzag stitch can be used. Some machines have a special stretch stitch, although this can be difficult to unpick. A flat zigzag seam will need to be pressed to one side to accommodate the width of the stitching.

① Place the two pieces of fabric with right sides facing and edges level, and pin and tack along the seamline.

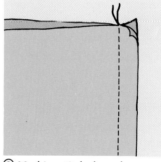

② Machine stitch along the seamline. Remove tacking, and press.

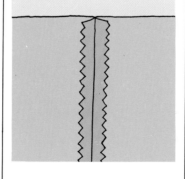

CROSSED SEAM

A crossed seam is formed when two pieces of fabric that each contain a flat seam are joined at right angles to the seams.
① Neaten the raw edges of the seams before joining the pieces together. With the right sides of the two pieces of fabric facing, pin along the seamline, ensuring that the crossed seams align by inserting a fine pin through both seams as shown.

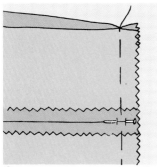

② After tacking and stitching the seam, trim the seam allowances diagonally to reduce any bulk. Remove the tacking and press the seam open.

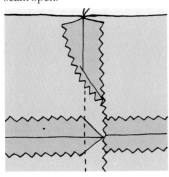

FRENCH SEAM

A French seam is a narrow seam which encloses the raw edges of the fabric so that fraying does not occur. It is normally used on fine, semi-transparent fabric or on medium-weight fabric that has a tendency to fray badly. Do not use this seam on heavy fabrics, as the effect will be bulky and unsightly. This seam is often used on baby garments and lingerie, and the finished seam should be no wider than 5mm ($\frac{1}{4}$in). It is always pressed to one side, towards the back of the garment.
① Place the two pieces of fabric with wrong sides facing. Pin, tack and stitch about 1cm ($\frac{3}{8}$in) from the raw edges. Trim both the seam allowances to 3mm ($\frac{1}{8}$in).

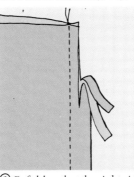

② Refold so that the right sides are together and the seam is at the edge. Pin, tack and stitch along the seam again, this time 5mm ($\frac{1}{4}$in) from the edge.

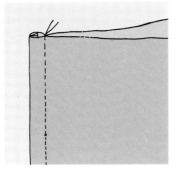

FLAT FELL SEAM

A flat fell seam is a very useful self-neatening seam which is used extensively where a strong seam is needed that will not fray. Use this seam on medium-weight fabrics such as cotton and linen, as it is rather bulky when used on heavy fabrics. Two rows of stitching show on one side of the seam and these can be in a contrasting colour. Denim jeans are usually put together using a flat fell seam, as it is durable.
① Place the two pieces of fabric with wrong sides facing. Pin, tack and stitch about 1.5cm ($\frac{5}{8}$in) from the raw edges. Trim one seam allowance to 5mm ($\frac{1}{4}$in).

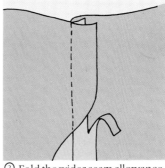

② Fold the wider seam allowance in half with the raw edge to the seamline. The narrower seam allowance is now neatly enclosed. Press the seam down flat and then tack to keep the folded edge in place. Stitch along the fold to finish.

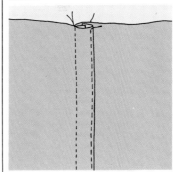

PLAIN SEAMS

TAPED SEAM

A taped seam is similar to a flat seam, but it is used where there are areas of particular strain, especially on garments. It incorporates seam binding or tape which should always be pre-shrunk to avoid the seam puckering after it is laundered. This seam is usually pressed open.

① Place the two pieces of fabric with right sides facing, and pin and tack along the seamline. Tack a length of seam binding or tape along the seamline. If you are taping a curved seam, ease the binding or tape carefully round the curve while you are tacking it.

② Turn the fabric over with the taped side facing down, and stitch close to the tacking. Remove tacking before pressing.

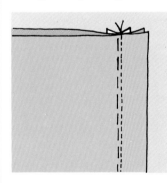

SELF-FINISHED SEAM

This seam is used where one piece of fabric is gathered and one is flat. It is also useful for fraying fabrics as the raw edges are enclosed, but it forms a rather bulky ridge and is only successful on lightweight fabrics.

① Place the two pieces of fabric with the right sides facing, with the gathered piece on top. Tack along seamline and stitch. Remove tacking, trim upper or gathered seam allowance only to 5mm (¼in).

② Fold the wider edge over twice, as shown, bringing it over to meet the line of stitching. Tack and press.

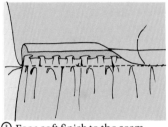

③ For a soft finish to the seam, hand stitch the fold, taking the stitches into the machined line, rather than through the fabric. Alternatively, machine stitch along close to the fold. This will give a harder ridge, but it will be more hard wearing.

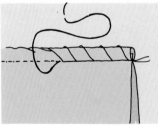

④ When using this seam on flimsy fabric, make the seam narrower by trimming down the wider seam allowance to 5mm (¼in), and the narrower one to 2mm (¹⁄₁₆in). Fold down as in step 2, and overcast over the edge by hand, bringing the needle through just above the line of stitching and pulling the stitches fairly tight.

CURVED SEAM

A curved seam is used to provide shaping, and it is used to join two pieces of fabric that differ in shape as one piece will generally be more curved than the other.

① Place the two pieces of fabric together with right sides facing, with the more curved piece on top. Pin together exactly on the seamline with the points of the pins facing outwards as shown, picking up a tiny piece of fabric each time. Ease the top piece into position and hold the seam over your hand to pin, keeping the curve even.

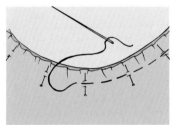

② Tack along the seamline with small stitches and remove the pins. If the fabric is quite stiff, you will need to clip the seam allowance as you work.

③ Keeping the more shaped piece on top, stitch carefully along the curve, following the tacked line closely. Trim seam allowance and clip further if necessary. Press this seam either open and neaten the edges separately, or to one side and neaten the edges together.

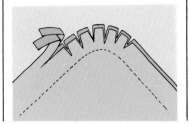

CORNER SEAM

A corner seam is used to provide shaping and is usually constructed using an ordinary flat seam. This seam is a little tricky to sew in order to keep the corner sharp and neat. If the seam will not be enclosed, neaten the edges of the fabric before beginning the seam.
① Mark the corner points on the fabric with tailor's tacks. With the right sides of the two pieces of fabric facing, pin along one side up to the corner with the pins at right angles to the seamline.

② Clip the top piece of fabric at the corner point. Stitch the pinned seam to the corner, leaving the point of the needle in the fabric.

③ Pivot the work round on the needle. Align both layers of fabric as shown, then pin the second side of the seam and stitch to the end. Remove the tailor's tack and press the seam flat.

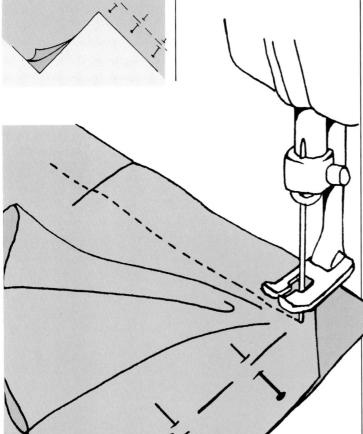

WELT SEAM

A welt seam is extremely strong and is suitable for use on almost all fabrics, apart from fine fabrics, which have a tendency to fray badly. A row of stitching shows on the right side and this can add interest to a plain fabric if a contrasting colour of thread is used.
① Place the two pieces of fabric together with right sides facing. Pin, tack and stitch along the seamline. Remove the tacking and press the seam to one side, depending on where you want the row of stitching to show.
② Open the pressed seam allowances and trim the underneath one to slightly less than 1cm (³⁄₈in). At this stage, neaten the edge of the wider seam allowance unless the item is to be lined.

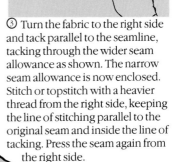

③ Turn the fabric to the right side and tack parallel to the seamline, tacking through the wider seam allowance as shown. The narrow seam allowance is now enclosed. Stitch or topstitch with a heavier thread from the right side, keeping the line of stitching parallel to the original seam and inside the line of tacking. Press the seam again from the right side.

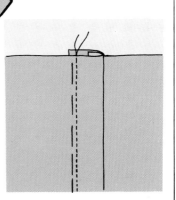

NARROW FINISH SEAM

A narrow finish seam is used only on lightweight or semi-transparent fabrics. It is an inconspicuous way of joining fine fabrics and can be finished either by hand or machine.

① Place the two pieces of fabric together with the right sides facing. Pin, tack and stitch along the seamline. Remove the tacking and press the seam to one side.

② To finish by machine, trim the seam allowances to 5mm ($\frac{1}{4}$in) and zigzag over both together.

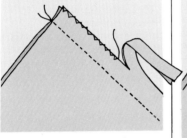

To finish by hand, fold the seam allowances in to meet each other, as shown. Tack the folds together, press and slipstitch neatly.

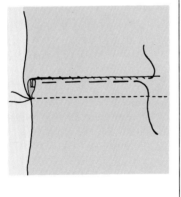

ROLLED SEAM

A rolled seam is used on fine fabrics and it is a self-neatening seam. It looks rather similar to a French seam, but only one row of stitching is used. Use rolled seams on loosely fitting garments only, as they could split when stretched.

① Place the two pieces of fabric together with the right sides facing and tack along the seamline. Trim one seam allowance down to within 3mm ($\frac{1}{8}$in) of the tacking. On a very fine fabric, also trim the wider allowance down slightly.

② Fold the wider seam allowance over once, and then fold it just over the tacked line. Tack through the fold along the seamline. Stitch along the edge of the fold, remove tacking, and press from the wrong side.

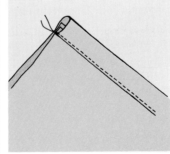

CHANNEL OR SLOT SEAM

A channel seam can be used on most types of fabric, but it will work best with a plain, fairly firm fabric. A backing strip is incorporated which shows between the seam edges. This can be cut from a matching or contrasting colour or a patterned fabric. Try to use the same weight of fabric for the backing strip as for the main item, or back a finer fabric with iron-on interfacing for added firmness. The width of the backing strip depends on the weight of the fabric and how much of it will be seen. Usually, the maximum amount which should show through is 5mm (¼in), but it could be larger to give a more decorative effect.

When adding this type of seam to a pattern piece, work the seam first on a larger piece of fabric, and then cut out the fabric from the pattern piece later.

① Turn in the raw edges of the two pieces of main fabric along the seamline. Tack, press and neaten the edges. Cut a bias strip of the contrasting fabric at least 3cm (1¼in) wide. Neaten the edges and mark the centre of the strip with a line of tacking.

② Tack one folded edge of the main fabric, right side up, to the strip, about 2mm (¹⁄₁₆in) from the centre. The top edge of the main fabric should be slightly lower than the edge of the backing strip, as shown. Tack the other folded edge in the same way, keeping both folds parallel. Work a row of diagonal tacking across the folds as shown.

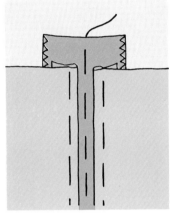

③ On the right side, stitch along the folds about 3mm (⅛in) away from the edge. Remove the tacking and press from the wrong side on a well-padded surface.

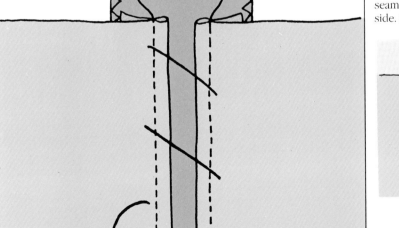

TOPSTITCHED SEAM

A plain flat seam can be decorated by topstitching over it in a matching or contrasting colour, or heavier weight of thread. The stitching can be on one side of the seam or both, and can be worked by hand or machine. Decorative machine stitches can also be used. Check the size of the seam allowance before you begin cutting out, and add a little extra if necessary. If you are topstitching along both sides of the seam, always stitch in the same direction or the stitching could pull the fabric and make it pucker.

① Make a flat seam, press and neaten the edges. Tack through the layers of fabric at the required distance from the seam, and machine on the right side close to the tacked lines as shown. Remove the tacking and press.

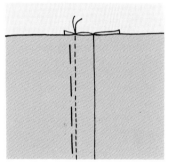

② To give a raised effect to the seam, cut narrow bias strips of fine fabric and insert them under the seam allowance on the wrong side. Finish the seam as above.

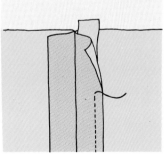

D E C O R A T I V E   S E A M S

INSERTION SEAM

An insertion seam is used to attach lengths of lace or braid to lingerie and garments made from lightweight fabrics. The insertions can be made almost anywhere on the garment and can be as wide or narrow as you like. They are added after the pattern pieces have been cut out as no extra seam allowance is needed.

① Mark the position of the insertion on the right side of the main fabric, using a line of tacking or tailor's tacks. Place one edge of the insertion along the markings and tack it in place. Holding the insertion flat to prevent puckering, tack it down along the second side.

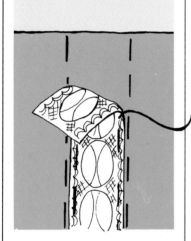

② Attach the insertion on the right side with straight, zigzag or machine embroidery stitches. Use a matching thread so the stitching is inconspicuous and keep the stitching as close to the edge as possible. Remove the tacking, then press from the wrong side on a well-padded surface.

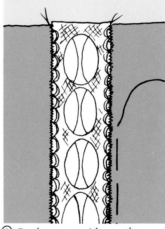

③ On the wrong side, cut the fabric away between the rows of stitching, using a sharp pair of scissors. Trim the edges and finish them by hand overcasting. When using a transparent insertion, roll the edges back to the main fabric and hand hem. This will prevent them from showing through on the right side and spoiling the look of the finished garment.

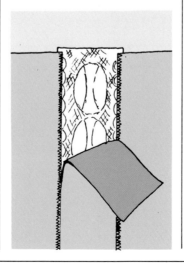

LAPPED SEAM

A lapped seam is simple to construct and relies on the use of a contrasting thread to add decoration. One side of the seam laps over the other and this seam can be used on any type of fabric.

① After deciding which way the seam will face, turn under the seam allowance on the top layer of fabric along the seamline. Tack along the fold and press. Place this on the second piece of fabric with the right sides uppermost, matching the seamlines, and tack in place.

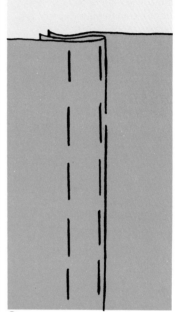

② Stitch along the fold on the right side using a straight, zigzag or machine embroidery stitch and a contrasting thread; take care to keep the line of stitching perfectly even.

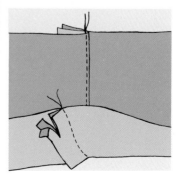

A faggoted seam is very decorative but not particularly strong, so avoid using this seam on garments that are going to be worn frequently. The two pieces of fabric are joined by hand embroidery, leaving a small gap between them. The gap can vary between 3mm ($\frac{1}{8}$in) on fine fabric and 1cm ($\frac{3}{8}$in) on wool or heavy cottons. Work a faggoted seam on a larger piece of fabric first and then cut out the pattern pieces.

① Mark the position of the faggoting on the right side of the fabric with a line of tacking. Cut the fabric on this line and press a narrow double hem to the wrong side along each edge. Hand stitch the hem on each piece.

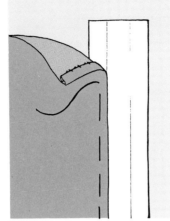

② With a pencil and ruler, mark parallel lines the required distance apart on a piece of typing paper or thin brown paper. These will act as guidelines to keep the fabric even while the embroidery is being worked. Tack one piece of fabric along the left-hand pencil line as shown, and then tack the second piece along the other line.

③ Join the edges with faggoting, using a suitable weight of embroidery thread for the type of fabric.

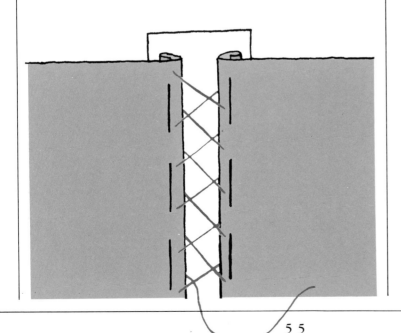

Piped seams are used on both garments and home furnishings to accentuate the construction lines. The piping can be left unfilled to give a soft look, or filled with a length of cord for a more pronounced line.
A matching or contrasting colour can be used for the piping fabric.
A piped seam is quite stiff, even when left unfilled, and is unsuitable for softly draped home furnishings or garments.

SOFT PIPED SEAM

① Cut bias strips of the piping fabric approximately 3cm (1¼in) wide and join them together into a long strip. Alternatively, ready-made bias binding could be used.
② Fold the strip in half lengthways with the wrong sides facing and press. Tack the folded strip along the seamline on the right side of one of the seam edges with the raw edges facing outwards, as shown.

③ Place the second piece of fabric over the strip with the right sides together. Tack through all the layers, turning the fabric back occasionally to check that the seamlines match. Stitch close to the tacking. Remove the tacking and press. Trim away any excess piping at the ends of the seam.

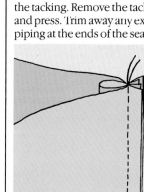

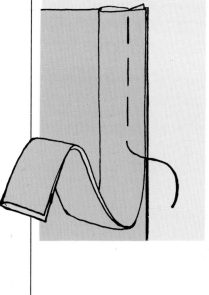

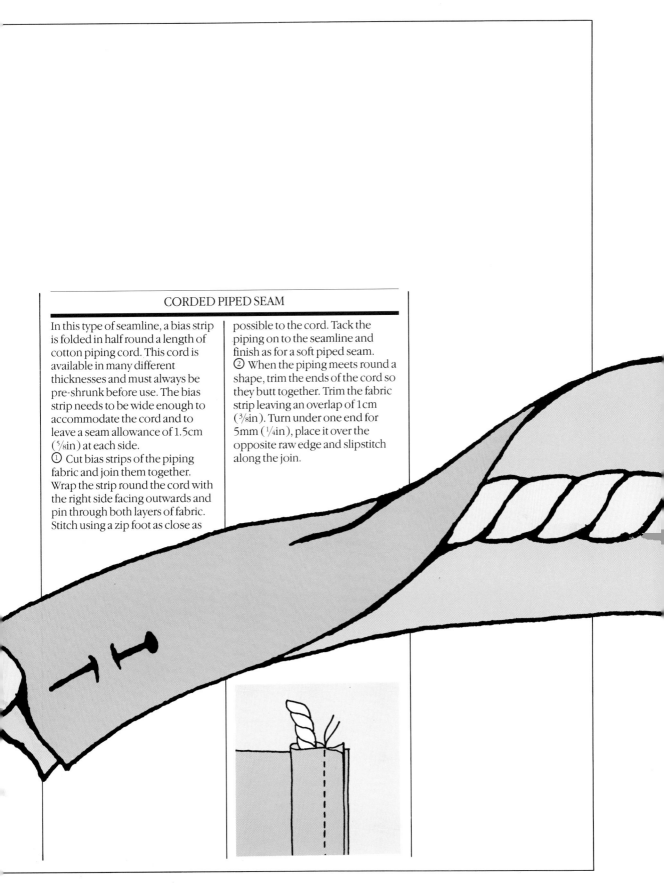

CORDED PIPED SEAM

In this type of seamline, a bias strip is folded in half round a length of cotton piping cord. This cord is available in many different thicknesses and must always be pre-shrunk before use. The bias strip needs to be wide enough to accommodate the cord and to leave a seam allowance of 1.5cm ($^5/_8$in) at each side.
① Cut bias strips of the piping fabric and join them together. Wrap the strip round the cord with the right side facing outwards and pin through both layers of fabric. Stitch using a zip foot as close as possible to the cord. Tack the piping on to the seamline and finish as for a soft piped seam.
② When the piping meets round a shape, trim the ends of the cord so they butt together. Trim the fabric strip leaving an overlap of 1cm ($^3/_8$in). Turn under one end for 5mm ($^1/_4$in), place it over the opposite raw edge and slipstitch along the join.

SPECIAL SEAMS

Special seams are used for particular types of fabric which can be a little tricky to sew, for example, stretch fabrics and velvet.

STRETCH FABRIC SEAM

Stretch fabric must be sewn with a stitch that allows the fabric to 'give', otherwise the stitching may break during use.

① Stitch as for a flat seam, using a narrow zigzag stitch, a special stretch stitch setting, or a narrow multi stitch (also called three-step zigzag or tricot stitch).

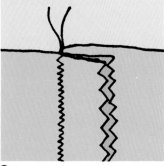

② If your machine has only a straight stitch setting, stretch the fabric gently with your hands as it passes under the needle. Use a smaller than normal stitch and polyester thread.

LACE SEAM

This seam is used on patterned lace to give an almost invisible join. Use a thread that matches the colour of lace perfectly.

① Cut out the lace with a slightly wider seam allowance than usual and mark the seamlines with tailor's tacks. With both pieces right side up, lap one piece over the other, taking care to match the seamlines exactly. Use a row of tacking near the seamline to mark out a stitching line, following the pattern of the lace as closely as possible.

② Work over the tacked line with a close machine zigzag stitch. Remove the tacking and carefully trim away the excess lace on both the top and the underneath piece. Press the join with the right side down on a well-padded surface.

VELVET SEAM

Use a velvet seam on any kind of pile fabric.
① Place the two pieces of fabric together with the right sides facing. Tack along the seamline following the direction of the pile. Do not fasten off the tacking thread.
② Stitch the seam in the same direction, cutting the tacking stitches as necessary to allow the top piece of fabric to move.

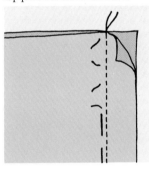

HAIRLINE SEAM

A hairline seam is used on fine fabrics where a normal seam turning would show through and look untidy. It can also be used for a full, gathered garment where a bulky seam would be unsightly.
① Place the fabric with the right sides facing. Pin and tack just outside the seamline.

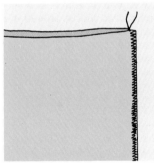

② Stitch along the seamline using a narrow, close zigzag stitch. Remove the tacking and trim the seam allowance close to the stitching.

NEATENING SEAMS

The raw edges that are left on the wrong side of those seams that are not self-neatening should be finished in order to stop the fabric from fraying. Cutting out the pattern pieces with a pair of pinking shears will usually be sufficient to prevent most closely woven and some knitted fabrics from fraying. However, if the item is going to be washed frequently or by machine, neaten the edges by one of the methods described below. Always neaten the edges of fabrics which look as if they are liable to fray.

MULTI STITCH

This stitch is produced on many swing needle machines. It is very stretchy, making it useful for finishing the edges on jersey, knits and other stretch fabrics. Work from the right side and multi stitch along each edge, keeping the row of stitches close to the edge, without taking the stitching over the edge. Press the seam open.

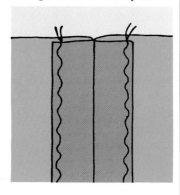

EDGE STITCHING

This is a quick and neat way of finishing the raw edges on light- and medium-weight fabrics. Fold under 3mm (1/8in) of the seam allowance and press the fold. With the right side uppermost, stitch close to the fold with a straight machine stitch and press the seam open.

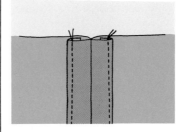

ZIGZAG STITCHING

A zigzag edged seam is ideal for finishing the raw edges on fabrics that fray badly. Set the machine to the appropriate stitch length and width of zigzag. Stitch along the right side of the edge so that the needle stitches once into the fabric and then once over the edge. Press the seam open.

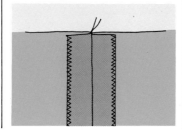

NEATENING BY HAND

Neaten the raw edges by working a row of overcasting along them. Leave the stitching quite loose as the fabric edges may curl and make a ridge if the stitching is too tight. Overcasting can be used on most types of fabric.

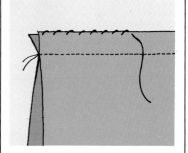

SEAM BINDING

Seam binding can be used to neaten the raw edges on heavy, bulky fabrics that fray. Fold the binding in half lengthways and enclose the raw edge within it. Pin, tack and stitch in place. When the seams are curved, use bias binding in preference to seam binding, as it will stretch around the curve.

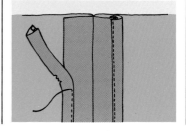

Unless a seam is a self-neatening seam, the seam allowance should be trimmed wherever the seam curves in order to leave a neat, flat seam. On heavy fabric, the seam allowance may also need to be graded to eliminated bulk.

NOTCHING

When the seam allowance finishes on the inside of a curve, cut out small 'V' shapes at regular intervals almost up to the line of stitching. This is called notching and it allows the fabric to fit into the curve, giving a smooth finish.

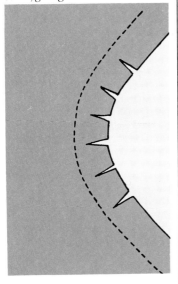

CLIPPING

When the seam allowance finishes on the outside of a curve, cut into it at frequent intervals almost up to the line of stitching. This is called clipping and it allows the fabric to spread out around the curve so that it does not pucker.

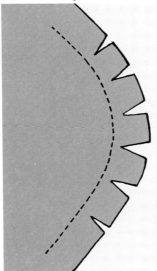

GRADING

Grading is used on seam allowances when bulk needs to be eliminated. This often happens where you have several thicknesses of fabric, such as on collars and cuffs. Trim the interfacing close to the line of stitching. Trim the under layer of fabric to within 3mm ($\frac{1}{8}$in) of the stitching, and then the outer layer to within 5mm ($\frac{1}{4}$in) of the stitching.

Fabric can be shaped in various ways, depending on the effect required. It can be cut and joined to create a shape, controlling any extra fullness by means of pointed folds called darts. It can be gathered or shirred into tucks and pleats.

The method of shaping used will influence the type of fabric required, and vice versa. A design using gathers or unpressed pleats will need a soft fabric such as silk or cotton jersey, which will drape easily. Crisp fabrics such as linen or cotton piqué can be shaped with darts, intricate seaming and pressed pleats. Heavy fabrics including woollen tweed, elephant cord and linen union will have to be shaped mainly by cutting and seaming, with the addition of darts. Fabrics with bright, bold patterns need careful attention and usually work best with a simple shape, which will show the pattern to full advantage.

Another factor to consider is the extra fabric required to make pleats, tucks and gathers. This could be important when you are intending to buy an expensive fabric such as pure silk. If you are designing an item rather than following a commercial pattern, remember to allow sufficient fabric for three times the width of each pleat. For gathers allow half as much fabric again to double the amount, depending on the fullness required.

DARTS

Darts are used to provide shaping and can be curved or straight, and single- or double-pointed. The length, width, shape and position of darts will depend on the design of the garment or item, and they may need to be altered to give a correct fit. Any corresponding darts should be realigned to match.

Darts are normally worked on the wrong side unless they are used as a decorative feature. Before stitching a dart, check the fit and adjust the position and shape of the darts as required. Darts should always taper to a fine point to fit well. Slashed darts are pressed flat and other types are pressed to one side, over an ironing ham if necessary. Always press darts before proceeding to the next stage of making up.

MAKING A SIMPLE DART

① Mark the position of the dart with tailor's tacks or a tracing wheel. Fold the dart in half, matching the markings carefully.

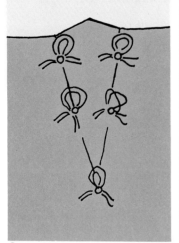

② Pin and tack the dart starting at the raw edge and tapering it to a fine point.
③ Check the fit and adjust the dart. Remove the tailor's tacks and stitch, starting at the raw edge. Reinforce the point by working a few reverse stitches. Press as appropriate.

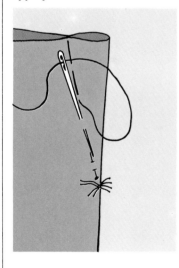

SPECIAL FINISHES FOR DARTS

Deep dart A dart which is made with a deep fold should be slashed along the fold to within 1.5cm (⅝in) of the point. Overcast the edges if the fabric is liable to fray, and then press the dart open.

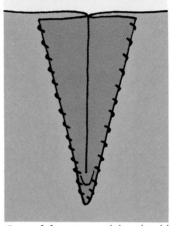

Curved dart A curved dart should be clipped along the curve, as shown. Reinforce the curve with a second line of stitching, then press to one side.

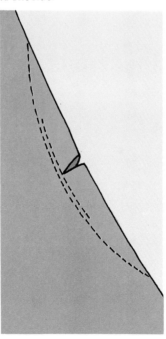

Contour dart A contour dart is pointed at both ends. After stitching the dart, clip it at the widest point almost up to the stitched line and work a second line of stitching along the curve as a reinforcement. Overcast the clipped edges if the fabric is liable to fray.

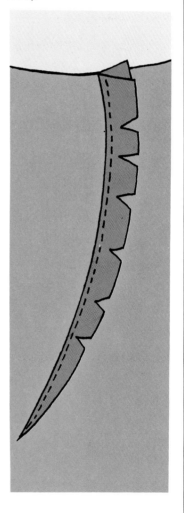

Gathering and shirring are both formed by drawing up a piece of fabric by means of rows of stitching. Gathering is worked near the edge of a piece of fabric which will then be joined to an ungathered piece. Frills are made by this method. Shirring is worked in a band across the fabric in the same way as smocking.

GATHERING

Gathering can be worked by hand with evenly spaced rows of running stitch or on a machine using the longest stitch length available. Use a long piece of thread for the running stitch to allow you to complete each section of stitching without a break.

① Work two rows of small running stitches or machine stitching 5mm (¼in) apart just outside the seamline. Do not fasten off the ends of the thread.

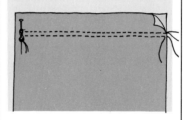

② Pull up the threads at each end of the stitching until the gathered section is the required width. Arrange the gathers evenly. Fasten the gathering threads by winding them round a pin, as shown.

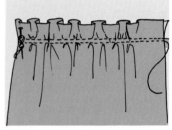

③ Pin the gathered fabric to the ungathered section placing the right sides together and the gathered fabric on the top. The pins should be at right angles to the stitching. Tack and then stitch along the seamline. A second row of stitching should be worked to reinforce the first if the gathering is at a point of strain, for example at the waistline of a dress. Remove the pins holding the gathering threads, snip the gathering threads at the centre and pull them out.

Fabric can be shirred by working multiple parallel rows of straight machine stitching, using the longest stitch length.

① Draw up the threads in the same way as for gathering.

② Fold back the side edges of the fabric and stitch to secure the ends shirring threads.

Fabric can also be shirred on the machine using a special elastic thread called shirring elastic. This can be either threaded into the bobbin or couched directly on to the fabric with a narrow zigzag stitch.

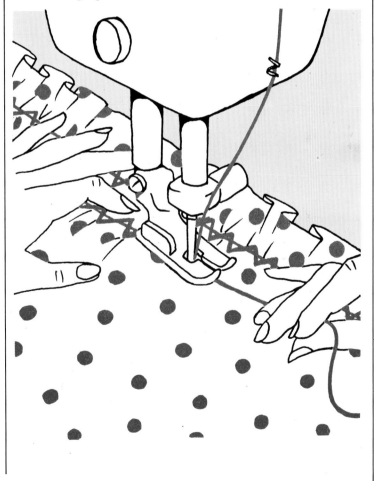

Pleats are folds made in fabric used to distribute fullness. There are three main types of pleats: knife pleats, box pleats and inverted pleats. On crisp fabrics, pleats are usually pressed and can be stitched to help them retain their shape in wear. Pleats on soft fabrics look best when they are left unpressed. It is essential to mark the position of pleats accurately so that each pleat takes up exactly the same amount of fabric and the fullness is evenly distributed.

KNIFE PLEATS

The folds of knife pleats face in the same direction along the whole pleated section.

① Mark the position of the pleats on the right side of the fabric with simplified tailor's tacks. Use a contrasting colour of thread for the fold lines and the pleat-edge lines.

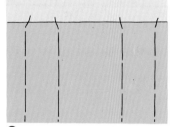

② Working from the right side, fold the pleats along the marked lines. Pin them in position with the pins at right angles to the folds. Secure the pleats with diagonal tacking stitch and remove the tailor's tacks.

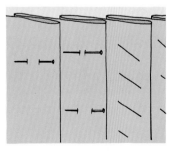

BOX PLEATS

Box pleats have two folds of equal width forming each pleat. The folds turn away from each other on the right side of the fabric with the underneath pleats meeting at the centre to form an inverted pleat on the wrong side. Box pleats are often used singly to add extra fullness, such as at the centre back of a shirt.

① Mark the position of the pleats on the right side of the fabric with simplified tailor's tacks. Use a contrasting thread for the fold lines and the pleat-edge lines.

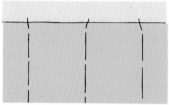

② Working from the right side, fold the pleats along the marked lines, as shown, and pin them in position at right angles to the folds. Secure the pleats with diagonal tacking stitch and remove the tailor's tacks.

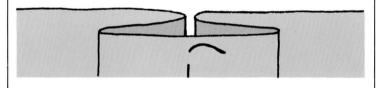

INVERTED PLEATS

Inverted pleats are the reverse of box pleats. The inverted pleats are on the right side of the fabric with the box pleats being formed on the wrong side. This type of pleat is often used on skirts and loose covers.

① Mark the pleats in the same way as for box pleats. Fold pairs of pleats towards each other, as shown.

② Pin the pleats in position at right angles to the folds and secure them with diagonal tacking stitch. Remove the tailor's tacks.

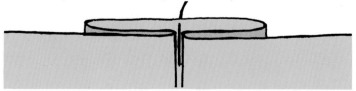

All pleats can be pressed, unpressed, or stitched. If the pleats are to be pressed or stitched down to the hem, finish the hem first. When making pressed pleats, use a damp pressing cloth between the iron and the pleats to avoid making the fabric shiny. Let the fabric dry thoroughly before removing the tacking stitches. For stitched pleats, first press the pleats in position, then stitch through the folds only close to the edge of each pleat using a matching thread.

STITCHING KNIFE PLEATS

Stitch the edge of each pleat 3mm (⅛in) from the fold and finish at the appropriate point down the pleat. Pull the threads through to the wrong side and fasten off securely. Take care to make the stitched lines all the same length.

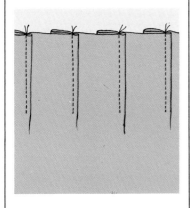

STITCHING INVERTED PLEATS

Stitch each pleat as shown, pivoting at the corners. Pull the threads through to the wrong side and fasten off securely.

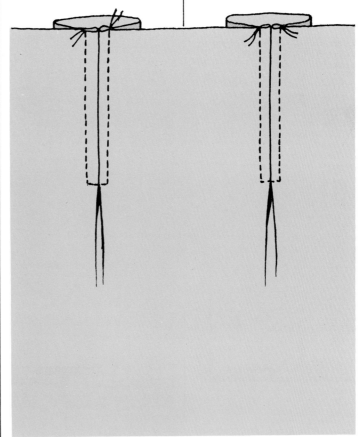

T U C K S

Tucks are really a narrow version of knife pleats. They can be made in different widths, and the narrowest tucks are known as pin tucks. Tucks can be placed horizontally or vertically and they are often used as a purely decorative feature on bodices and yokes. Vertical tucks can be stitched down to the hem or seamline, or the fabric can be released at a certain point to give fullness to a skirt or smock. Wide horizontal tucks are often found on children's clothes, as they can be unpicked to lengthen a skirt or sleeves.

TUCKS

① Mark the position of the tucks with simplified tailor's tacks, using two colours of thread to denote the different lines.

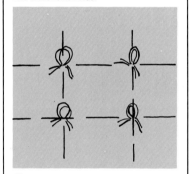

② Fold the tucks, matching the markings, and keeping the width of the tucks even. Pin and tack them in position. Stitch along each tuck and remove the tacking threads. Decorative pin tucks can also be worked on fine fabrics using a twin needle, pin tuck foot and two colours of thread.

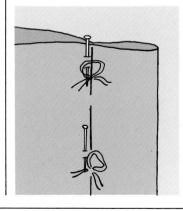

Finishing the hem is usually the last stage in making a garment or item for the home. Hems are nearly always hand stitched to give a neat finish, but a machine stitched edge is occasionally used on a narrow hem. Use a suitable stitch and take care not to pucker the fabric by pulling the thread too tightly when stitching.

Match seam and centre lines carefully and trim down the seam allowance under the hem to avoid unsightly bulges. The allowance left for a hem depends on its position and on the type of fabric being stitched. Heavy fabrics such as woollen tweed and furnishing fabrics need a deep hem so that the extra weight will help the fabric to hang well. Sleeves and lightweight fabrics will only require a narrow hem. Allow bias cut garments to hang at least overnight before marking the hem level as the fabric may drop unevenly.

MARKING THE HEM LINE

It is best to have help when marking the hem line on a skirt or dress. Use a hem marker or a metre ruler and tailor's chalk to measure an even distance from the floor. If help is not at hand, pin up the hem and try on the garment in front of a full length mirror. Note any alterations, remove the garment and re-pin the hem. You may have to repeat this procedure several times before the hem is finally neat and level. Alternatively hand-operated hem markers are available which simplify this process.

To mark the hem line on curtains, hang them on the curtain rail overnight, then measure an even distance from the floor using a metre ruler and chalk. Pin up the hem, then re-hang the curtains to check that the length is correct and the pattern is level.

TURNING THE HEM

Fold the hem along the chalk line and pin it up, placing the pins at right angles to the folded edge. Check that the hem is level and make any further adjustments at this stage. Tack the hem 5mm (¼in) above the folded edge and press it to sharpen the crease. Cut away any surplus fabric to make the hem the correct depth and trim any seam allowances inside the hem by half.

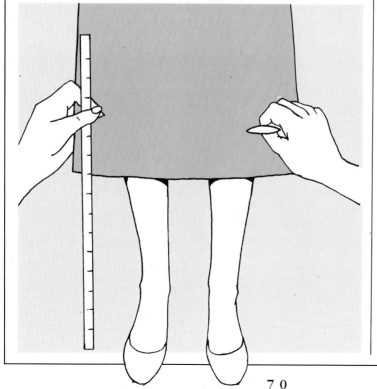

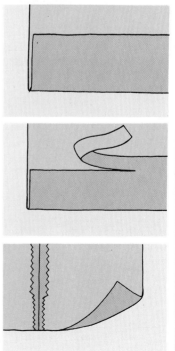

The shape of the item as well as the weight and type of fabric will determine which method of finishing to choose. Always finish hems by hand if an invisible finish is desired on the right side of the item.

PLAIN HEM

This method of finishing a hem is suitable for a straight hem on light- and medium-weight fabrics.
① Fold 5mm (¼in) under along the raw edge and press.
② Pin the hem edge in place, tack and finish with hem stitch. Remove the tacking and press the hem.

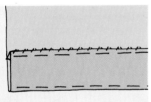

EDGE-STITCHED HEM

An edge-stitched hem is suitable for articles that are laundered frequently and for linings. Use this method for finishing a straight hem on most weights of fabric.
① Fold 5mm (¼in) under along the raw edge and machine stitch near the edge of the fold.
② Press, pin and tack the hem into place. Finish with slip stitch. Remove the tacking and press the hem.

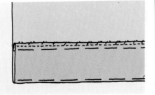

BLIND-STITCHED HEM

This hem can be used on any straight hem and it is particularly suitable for use on curtains. Use either straight or bias binding to enclose the raw edge.
① Sew the binding 5mm (¼in) from the raw edge of the hem using a narrow zigzag stitch. Press the binding.
② Pin the hem edge in place, tack and finish with blind hem stitch. Remove the tacking and press the hem.

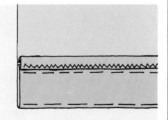

HERRINGBONE HEM

Use a herringbone hem on both loosely woven and heavy-weight fabrics. The raw edge should be cut with pinking shears or enclosed with bias binding before it is stitched. This hem can also be used on stretch fabrics if your machine does not have a zigzag setting.
① Pink the raw edge or attach the binding as for a blind-stitched hem. Press, pin and tack the hem in place.
② Stitch the hem using herringbone stitch, working from left to right. Remove the tacking and press.

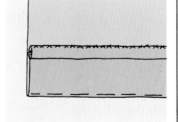

ZIGZAG HEM

A zigzag hem is used on stretch fabrics and knits. It prevents fraying and has the same amount of 'give' as the fabric.
① Work a row of narrow machine zigzag or multi stitch (three- step zigzag or tricot stitch) close to the raw edge. Press and trim close to the stitching with a pair of sharp scissors.

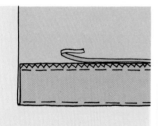

② Pin, tack and finish with blind hem stitch. Remove the tacking and press the hem.

FLARED HEM

A flared hem is used mainly on garments to finish the hem of a flared or gored skirt. The fullness of the skirt hem is controlled by gathering the edge slightly to ease in the fullness.
① Work running stitches 5mm (¼in) from the raw edge. Pin up the hem, matching centre and seamlines. Draw the running stitches up to ease the fullness and fit the skirt shape.
② Shrink out the fullness using a steam iron. Remove the pins and stitch a length of bias binding to the hem, placing it over the gathering thread.
③ Pin and tack the hem in place and press, shrinking the bias binding to the curve. Finish with blind hem stitch. Remove the tacking and press.

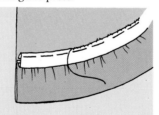

CIRCULAR HEM

A circular hem should be quite narrow so that it lies perfectly flat. Always hang a garment with a circular skirt overnight at least before finishing the hem.
① Mark the hem line and trim away any excess fabric, leaving a hem of about 1.5cm (⅝in). Pin, tack and stitch a length of bias binding 5mm (¼in) from the raw edge, taking care not to stretch the binding as you stitch.
② Press the binding and then fold the fabric along the marked line. Pin, tack and press, then finish with blind hem stitch or slip stitch. Remove the tacking and press the hem.

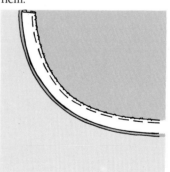

Finish the corners on hems so they are sharp and square by mitring or facing them. Mitred corners give a good finish to tablecloths and bedcovers, while faced hems are usual on garments such as coats and jackets.

MACHINE-STITCHED HEM

A narrow, machine-stitched hem is useful as it is quick to sew and strong. The stitching is visible on the right side, so care should be taken to keep the line of stitching straight. This hem can be stitched with a straight stitch foot as described below, or by using a narrow hemmer foot.
① Trim the hem allowance to 5mm ($\frac{1}{4}$in). Fold 3mm ($\frac{1}{8}$in) then another 3mm ($\frac{1}{8}$in) over to the wrong side and press.
② Tack along the centre of the hem, and then stitch close to the edge.

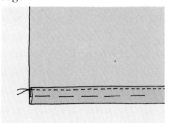

MITRED CORNERS

Hems with mitred corners can be either hand or machine stitched.
① Turn under the raw edges of the fabric and then fold the hem to the wrong side. Press it in position and open out the fabric. At the corner point of the hem fold, draw a diagonal line across the wrong side of the fabric with tailor's chalk. Cut off the corner of the fabric 5mm ($\frac{1}{4}$in) outside this line.
② With the right sides of the fabric facing and the raw edges turned under, fold the corner. Stitch along the marked diagonal line. Turn the corner right side out, press and finish the hem as desired.

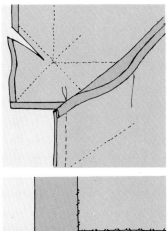

FACED CORNER

A hem with a faced corner is usually finished by hand.
① Neaten the edge of the facing by zigzag stitching, or by folding 5mm ($\frac{1}{4}$in) to the wrong side and machine stitching close to the edge. Pin, tack and finish the hem to the required depth.

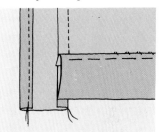

② Turn the facing back over the finished hem. Slip stitch the lower edge of facing to the hem, and then slip stitch the side of the facing to the hem to secure it.

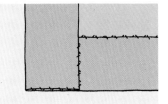

BINDINGS

Binding is a way of finishing a raw edge by enclosing it in a strip of fabric. A contrasting colour, pattern or weight of fabric is often used for the binding which can make it into a striking decorative feature.

Binding can be either single or double, except on heavy fabrics when single binding should be used. Single binding can be bought ready for use in a variety of colours and widths.

Binding strips can be cut from any type of fabric, although light- and medium-weight fabrics will give the best results. Leftover scraps of fabric provide a good source of binding, but if long lengths are required, buy extra fabric to avoid too many joins. The strips should be cut on the bias of the fabric, rather than along the grain, so that they will stretch easily round curves and fold over smoothly without twisting.

CUTTING THE BIAS STRIPS

For single binding, cut strips twice the required width plus a seam allowance on both sides of approximately 5mm ($^1/_4$in). Double binding should be four times the finished width plus the two seam allowances of 5mm ($^1/_4$in).

① Straighten the edges of the fabric by pulling the cross threads. Use the selvedge as one of the straight edges if you are cutting the binding from a length of fabric.

② Lay the fabric out flat and then fold it over with a straight edge to the selvedge, as shown. The diagonal fold is on the true bias of the fabric.

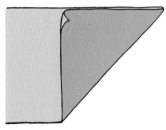

③ Pin along the diagonal, leaving the fold free, and cut along the fold. Mark a line the required distance from the fold and parallel to it. Cut along the line to give the first pair of strips. Continue marking and cutting in this way, moving the pins away from the edge each time.

JOINING THE BIAS STRIPS

Join the strips end to end, as shown, to form a strip 10cm (4in) longer than you need. The ends can be machine stitched 5mm ($^1/_4$in) from the edge, but a neater way is to work a line of back stitch by hand.

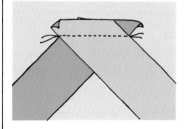

APPLYING SINGLE BINDING

① Place one edge of the bias strip right side down on to the right side of the fabric to be bound, allowing 2cm ($^3/_4$in) of binding to extend over the raw edge as shown. Take a 5mm ($^1/_4$in) seam allowance on the binding and a normal one on the fabric. Pin across the strip at intervals along the length. Tack the binding in position.

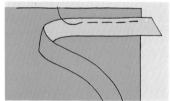

② With the bias strip on top, stitch along the seamline. Remove the tacking and press the stitching. Trim the seam allowance to slightly less than the finished width of the binding. On the right side, press the binding over the raw edge.

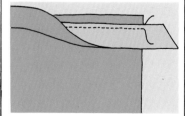

③ With the wrong side of the fabric facing, turn under 5mm ($^1/_4$in) of the binding and bring the fold on to the stitching. Tack the

binding into position in two sections, working from the centre outwards.
④ Hem into the machined line, picking up stitches about 5mm (¹/₄in) apart. Press lightly, taking care not to flatten the binding.

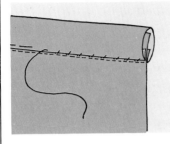

APPLYING DOUBLE BINDING

① Fold the bias strip in half with the wrong side inside and press it lightly. Tack the raw edges of the double strip to the fabric to be bound and proceed exactly as for single binding, until step 3 is reached.

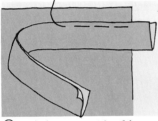

② With the wrong side of the fabric facing, roll the fold of the binding over to meet the stitched line. Tack it in position in two sections, working from the centre outwards. Hem into the stitching and press lightly.

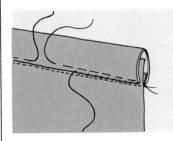

JOINING SINGLE AND DOUBLE BINDING

When binding a continuous edge such as an armhole, always make the final join in an inconspicuous place.
① Tack the bias strip in position, leaving 10mm (³/₈in) unstitched at the beginning and 20mm (³/₄in) overlapping at the end.

② Fold back the surplus 10mm (³/₈in) at the beginning of the strip and lay the other end on top, as shown, to overlap the folded end.
③ Tack the ends to the fabric along the seamline. Apply the binding in the normal way.

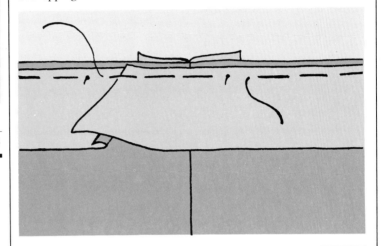

FLAT FINISH BINDING

Single binding can be applied to a raw edge in such a way that it is almost invisible from the right side, giving a neat, flat edge.
① Follow steps 1 and 2 for applying single binding.
② Turn under the 5mm (¹/₄in) seam allowance and fold the binding over to the wrong side, taking it past the line of stitching, as shown.
③ Tack the edge in position and slip stitch to hold it down. Press lightly from the wrong side.

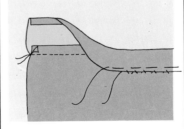

NARROW FINISH BINDING

This method of applying single binding gives a very neat finish when the main fabric is much heavier than the binding strip.
① Follow steps 1 and 2 for applying single binding.
② Trim both seam allowances down to 2mm (¹/₁₆in). Fold the free edge of the binding over to the wrong side without turning under the raw edge. Working from the right side, tack below the join.
③ Stitch on the edge of the binding or along the seamline using a zip foot and a machine straight stitch.

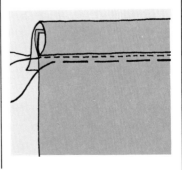

Three types of zip fasteners are available: standard zips which can be used on most garments, concealed zips which lie neatly inside a seam, and open-ended zips which are used on jackets and sleeping bags.

Zips are made in various weights and materials for different types of fabric, with the heaviest weight being the strongest in use. Match the colour of zip to the fabric you are using, or use one a shade darker. Always use a nylon zip on synthetic fabrics, as one with cotton tapes may shrink during laundering. Metal zips have nickel alloy teeth attached to a coloured cotton twill tape. Lightweight nylon zips are neat and unobtrusive, but not as strong as a metal zip. Open-ended zips for sleeping bags are often made of heavy nylon because they wash well and do not rust.

GENERAL RULES

Follow these rules when inserting a zip to obtain a professional finish.
① Match the zip length to the size of the opening.
② Check that the garment fits correctly before inserting the zip.
③ Neaten and press the seam before inserting the zip.
④ Pre-shrink the zip to prevent puckering if the item is to be washed rather than dry cleaned.

⑤ If the zip is too long, shorten it at the botton by oversewing over the zip teeth 2.5cm (1in) below the required length and cutting off the surplus.

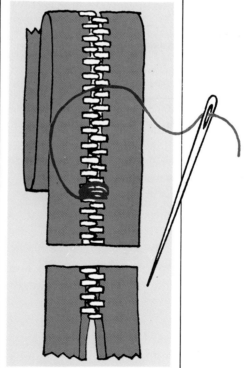

⑥ Pin upwards from the bottom of the zip wherever possible.
⑦ Use a zip foot when you are machine stitching.
⑧ Neaten the ends of the zip tape after insertion.

The easiest method of inserting a standard zip is to place it in the centre of the seam with an equal amount of fabric on each side.

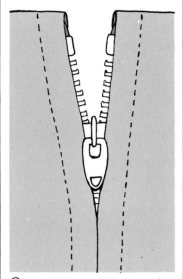

① Press the neatened seam and pin and tack the seam allowances together along the fold lines. Mark the end of the opening with a pin.
② Pin the zip in position with the teeth centred over the seam. Insert the pins at right angles to the zip, changing the direction of each alternate pin.

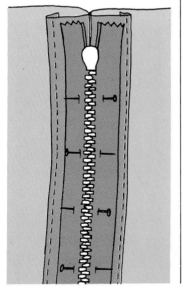

③ Tack 5mm (¼in) from the zip teeth and remove the pins. Stitch close to the tacking on the right side using a zip foot. Begin at the top and stitch down one side, pivot the fabric and stitch across the bottom and then continue up the other side. Alternatively, stitch the zip in by hand using a tiny half back stitch and double thread. Remove the tacking and neaten the ends of the zip tape.

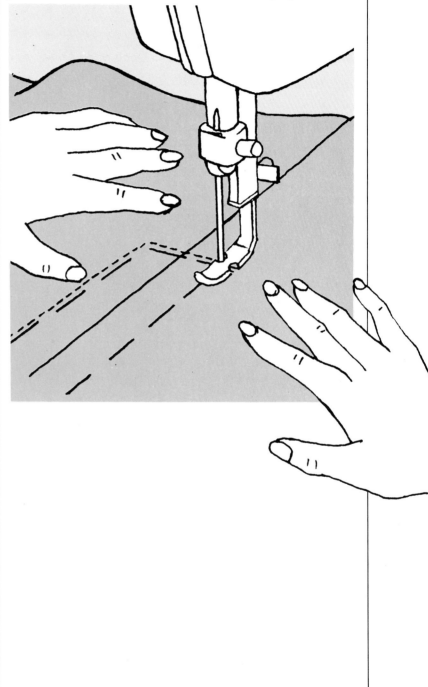

ZIP FASTENERS

A LAPPED STANDARD ZIP

A lapped zip lies behind a flap formed by the seam allowance on one side of the seam. Side zips on garments are usually lapped so that the flap faces towards the back of the garment.

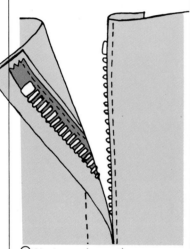

① Neaten and press the seam. Working from the right side, place the zip under the seam opening. Pin and tack one edge close to the teeth of the zip, as shown.
② Lap the opposite seam allowance over the zip teeth, making sure that they are completely covered. Pin and tack in position 1 cm (³/₈in)from the fold.
③ Stitch by hand or machine as for a centred standard zip, step 3.

A CONCEALED ZIP

A concealed zip is almost invisible and is used on tailored dresses where a standard zip could spoil the line of the garment. All that is visible on the right side is a plain seam and the pull tab. A concealed zip is always stitched in place before the seam is stitched.

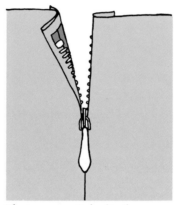

The tapes are stitched to the seam allowances of the garment pieces using a special concealed zip foot so that none of the stitching shows on the right side. The special zip foot must be the one recommended for the brand of zip that is being used.

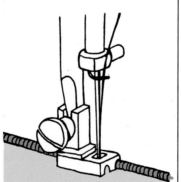

① Neaten the raw edges of the fabric and mark the seamlines with a line of tacking. Open the zip and press the tapes carefully so that the coils stand away from the tape. This will ensure that the zip will feed smoothly through the foot.
② Place the open zip face down on the right side of one garment piece. Position one coil on the seamline with the zip tape over the seam allowance, as shown. Pin or tack in position if necessary.

Fit the right-hand groove of the special foot over the coil and stitch as far as the tab of the zip.

③ Pin the unstitched tape face down to the right side of the other garment piece, centring the coil on the marked seamline. Stitch in place, this time using the left-hand groove of the foot.

④ Close the zip, then pin and tack the remainder of the seam in the usual way. Replace the special foot with an ordinary zip foot positioned to the left of the needle. Lower the needle into the fabric slightly above and to the left of the previous stitching. Stitch the seam.

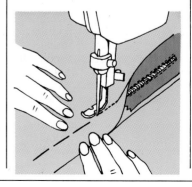

An open-ended zip should be inserted before any facings or hems are begun. This type of zip is usually centred with the teeth either concealed like a standard zip or exposed for a decorative finish.

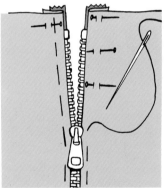

① Neaten and press the raw edge. Pin and tack the seam allowances together along the fold lines.
② Pin the zip in position with the teeth centred over the seam. Insert the pins at right angles to the zip, changing the direction of each alternate pin.

③ Tack approximately 6mm (¼in), or 1cm (⅜in) on heavy-weight zips, from the zip teeth and remove the pins. Stitch close to the tacking on the right side using a zip foot. Begin at the top and stitch down one side of the zip. Stitch the second side in the same direction. Alternatively, if you are using this type of zip on a lightweight garment, stitch the zip in by hand using half back stitch and double thread for strength. Remove the tacking.

Depending on the position of the zip, the tape ends may be exposed after insertion. In many cases, one end of the zip will eventually be covered by a facing, hem or waistband and need not be neatened. Exposed tape ends should be attached to the seam allowance with a row of blanket stitch. This will prevent the tape from rolling up and making a ridge.

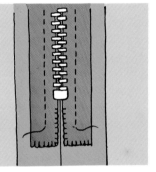

Finish the base of the zip opening by working a small bar tack by hand on the right side. If this would spoil the look of the finished item, work the bar tack on the wrong side just below the teeth of the zip.

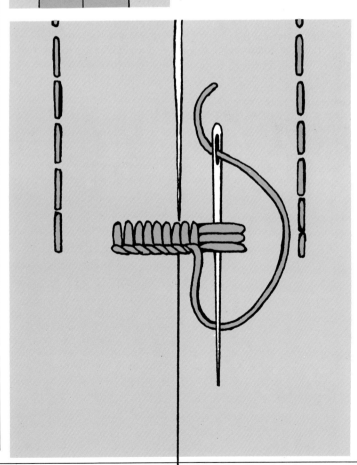

BUTTON OPENINGS

Overlapped openings fastened by buttons are found mainly on garments. Shirts, jackets and coats usually have a buttoned fastening on the front which can be decorative as well as functional. Small openings, especially those on children's garments, can also be buttoned for easy access.

Buttonholes can be worked successfully on all fabrics providing that the right type of buttonhole is made. Button loops are much more decorative and can be substituted for buttonholes if appropriate to the style of the garment. They are also useful when a single button is necessary, for example on a waistband. Button loops suit an edge-to-edge opening particularly well, but like buttonholes, they can also be used for an overlapped opening.

BUTTONHOLES

There are three methods of making buttonholes: machine worked, hand worked and bound. Always make the buttonholes before attaching the buttons. Horizontal buttonholes are used on the front of garments and at points of strain such as cuffs and waistbands. Vertical buttonholes should be confined to fastening loosely fitting garments and as a decorative feature because the buttons tend to come undone if the opening is put under strain.

Calculate the size of the buttonhole by measuring the diameter of the button and then allowing a little extra for the thickness of both the button and the fabric. After calculating the size, make a trial buttonhole on a spare piece of fabric in case any adjustments are needed. When marking the length of the buttonholes, use an adjustable marker set to the right measurement or a small strip of card cut to size.

MACHINE-WORKED BUTTONHOLES

Machine-worked buttonholes are suitable for most types of fabric and they are quick and easy to work. Work this type of buttonhole after all the other stages of the garment are completed.
① Mark the position and size of the buttonholes with tailor's chalk. To prevent fraying, press a rectangle of hemming web underneath each buttonhole between the garment and the facing.
② Using a buttonhole foot, stitch round the buttonhole following the instructions in your sewing machine handbook. Cut through the centre of the buttonhole using a small, extremely sharp pair of scissors.

HAND-WORKED BUTTONHOLES

Hand-worked buttonholes are a little tricky to work, but with practice a neat finish can be obtained. If you enjoy hand sewing, you will probably choose this type of buttonhole as it is suitable for all types of fabric. Choose a weight of thread to match the fabric and work the buttonholes after all the other stages of the garment have been completed.

① Mark the position and size of the buttonhole with lines of tacking, as shown. This is preferable to marking with chalk, as the tacking keeps the layers of fabric together while you are working the buttonhole. Insert a pin at each end of the buttonhole and cut a slit between the pins using a sharp pair of scissors. Remove the pins.

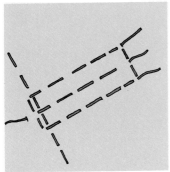

② On a horizontal buttonhole, stitch along the lower edge of the slit towards the edge of the garment using buttonhole stitch.

③ At the end of the slit, work five stitches in a semi-circle to accommodate the shank of the button. These stitches should be slightly shorter than those already worked. Work along the second side of the slit in the same way as the first.

④ Work a bar of satin stitch across the end of the buttonhole to the depth of both rows of buttonhole stitch. For a more hard-wearing buttonhole, work a bar tack instead of satin stitch. Fasten off the thread on the wrong side of the garment.

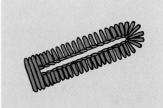

⑤ On a vertical buttonhole, work round the slit in the same way, but replace the semi-circular stitches with a satin stitch bar.

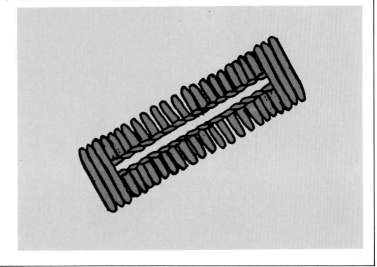

BOUND BUTTONHOLES

Bound buttonholes are used on light- and medium-weight fabrics and they look extremely neat and professional when worked correctly. The openings are bound with a strip of matching fabric and the first five stages should be completed after interfacing, but before the fabric facing is attached. Finish off the backs of the buttonholes after the garment is completed.

① Mark the position and size of the buttonholes with lines of tacking or chalk. Cut rectangles of fabric on the straight grain at least 3cm (1¼in) wider and longer than the buttonhole. Place the right side of the rectangle over the position, mark on the right side of the garment and tack in place.

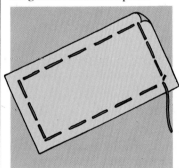

② Re-mark the buttonhole length on the rectangle. Work a rectangle of stitching around the position mark. The rectangle should be the same length as the buttonhole and three or four machine stitches wide. Work the final stitches over the first ones and cut off the thread ends. Remove the tacking and press.

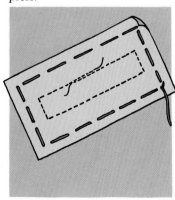

③ Cut a slit along the centre of the stitched rectangle, as shown, and clip into the corners up to the stitching. Press the sides of the fabric rectangle towards the slit.

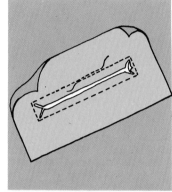

④ Push the rectangle through the slit to the wrong side. Manipulate the fabric until two folds of equal width fill the buttonhole opening, and tack the rectangle to the garment, as shown. Press and then diagonally tack the folds together at the centre of the buttonhole.

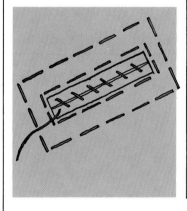

⑤ On the wrong side, the rectangle has formed an inverted pleat at each end of the opening. Hold the pleats in position with small bar tacks and remove the tacking stitches. Attach the sides of the rectangle to the garment with small pieces of hemming web. Press and then finish the remaining stages of the garment.

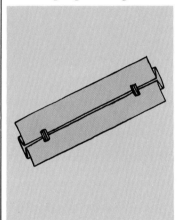

⑥ When the garment is complete, a fabric facing will cover the back of the buttonholes. Tack round the buttonholes on the right side of the garment, taking the stitches through the facing. Mark each end of the buttonhole on the wrong side by stabbing a pin through from the front.

⑦ On the wrong side, cut a slit in the facing between the pins and remove them. Turn the raw edge under with the point of a needle and hem round to make an oval shape, as shown. Press the buttonholes on the right side and remove the tacking.

Button loops are more decorative than buttonholes and they work particularly well on edge-to-edge openings. The loops can be made singly or in strips, and they are inserted between the main piece of fabric and the facing. The loops are made from bias strips which are stitched and then turned right side out to form rouleau tubing. The loops can be self coloured or made in a contrasting colour and type of fabric for extra effect.

MAKING ROULEAU TUBING

① Cut a bias strip of fabric the required length, joining several shorter strips if necessary. Fold the strip with the right side facing and stitch along it 3 to 5mm (¹/₈ to ¹/₄in) from the fold. The distance from the fold depends on the weight of the fabric, so you may need to work a small sample piece first to make sure that the strip can be turned without splitting. Trim the seam allowances to minimize bulk.

② Slide a rouleau needle into the tube and secure the eye to the seam allowance with a few stitches. Ease the tube gently back over the eye of the needle, as shown, and pull the needle through to turn the tubing right side out.

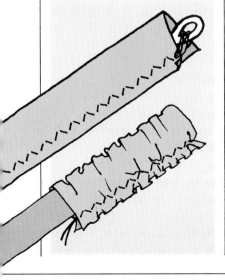

ATTACHING BUTTON LOOPS

Measure the diameter of the button and cut the rouleau tubing into sections, allowing sufficient length to fit round the button plus the seam allowance at each end.

① Mark the position for the loops on the seamline on the right side of the garment. Pin the loops in place and attach them with a row of stitching just inside the seam allowance.

② With right sides of the fabric together, pin and tack the facing in position. Stitch along the seamline. Fold the facing back to expose the loops and press it into position. Slipstitch the facing in place.

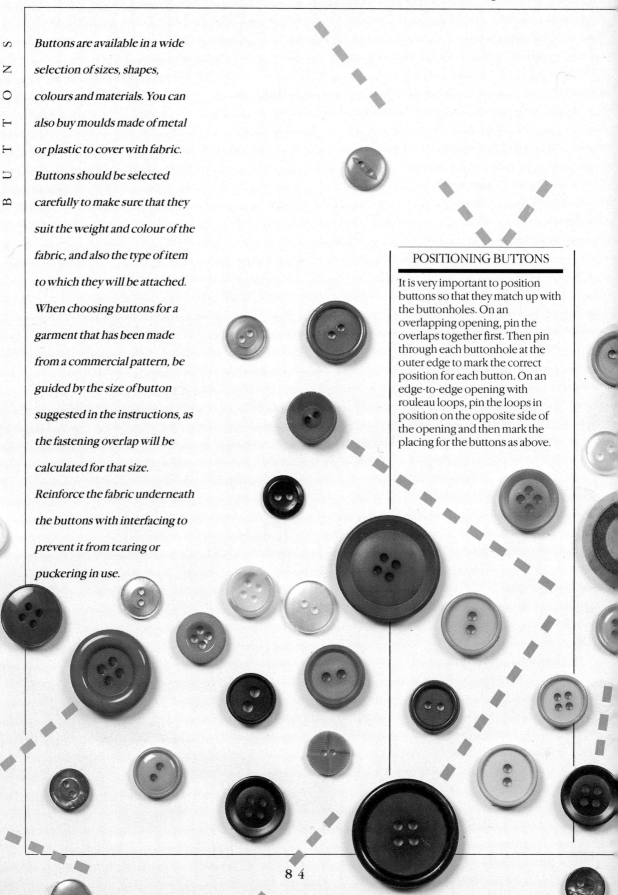

BUTTONS

Buttons are available in a wide selection of sizes, shapes, colours and materials. You can also buy moulds made of metal or plastic to cover with fabric. Buttons should be selected carefully to make sure that they suit the weight and colour of the fabric, and also the type of item to which they will be attached. When choosing buttons for a garment that has been made from a commercial pattern, be guided by the size of button suggested in the instructions, as the fastening overlap will be calculated for that size. Reinforce the fabric underneath the buttons with interfacing to prevent it from tearing or puckering in use.

POSITIONING BUTTONS

It is very important to position buttons so that they match up with the buttonholes. On an overlapping opening, pin the overlaps together first. Then pin through each buttonhole at the outer edge to mark the correct position for each button. On an edge-to-edge opening with rouleau loops, pin the loops in position on the opposite side of the opening and then mark the placing for the buttons as above.

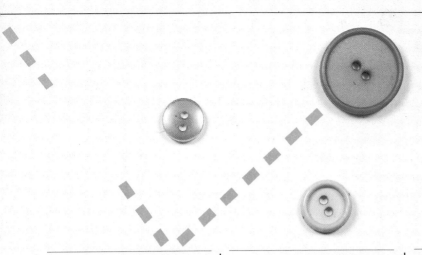

ATTACHING THE BUTTONS

Sew-through buttons are made with two or four holes right through the centre, and shank buttons have a metal or plastic loop underneath the surface of the button. They are stitched on according to their construction. All buttons should be stitched on securely using a strong, matching thread. Some 'give' should be left in the thread to allow the buttonhole to close under the button without distorting the fabric.

SEW-THROUGH BUTTONS

① Knot the thread and make two or three small stitches underneath the button to hide the knot. Stitch in and out of the holes over a pin, as shown, leaving the thread fairly loose under the button.

② Wind the thread round a few times between the button and the fabric to form a shank before taking it through to the wrong side. Fasten the thread off securely with two or three back stitches.

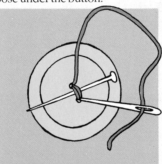

SHANK BUTTONS

① Secure the thread as for a sew-through button. Hold the button at right angles to the fabric and then stitch through the loop of the button and the fabric several times.

② Take the thread through to the wrong side and fasten off securely with two or three back stitches.

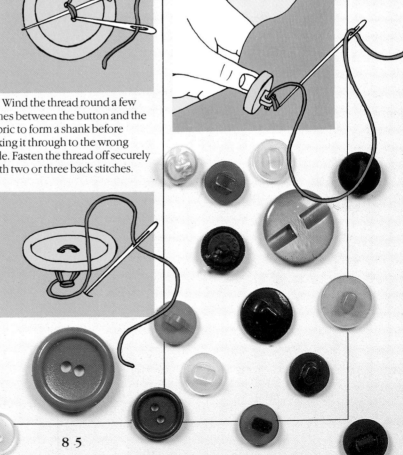

HOOKS AND EYES

Hooks and eyes are useful where an extra fastening is needed on an overlap or an edge-to-edge opening, for example, at a neckline or on a waistband. Hooks and bars are also available and are sewn on in the same way as hooks and eyes. Both types of fastening are made in black or silver coloured metal.

① Place the hook on the underside of the overlap 3mm to 1cm (¹/₈ to ³/₈in) in away from the edge so that the eye or bar is concealed when fastened. Attach it to the fabric by working close blanket stitch through the two loops at the end of the hook. Oversew the neck of the hook to the fabric to keep it flat.

② Position the eye to match on the other side of the opening and attach it with buttonhole stitch worked through the two smaller loops.

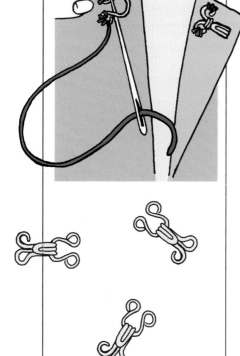

PRESS STUDS

Press studs can be used on most overlapping openings, providing that there is not much strain, as they can come undone easily. They are useful for fastening items such as cushion covers, and for attaching collars that need to be washed separately from the garment. They are usually made from black or silver coloured metal, but tiny press studs are also available in transparent plastic. The ball stud is usually placed on the right side of the underlap, with the socket on the under side of the overlap.

① Mark the position of the ball stud and sew it in place by working four or more stitches into each hole.

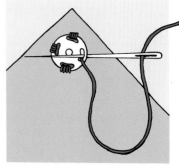

② Mark the position of the socket by aligning the two parts of the press stud and then putting a needle through the centres of both studs. Sew on the socket in the same way as the ball stud.

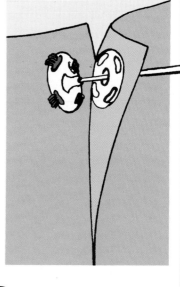

TOUCH AND CLOSE FASTENING

Touch and close is a versatile fastening strip with many applications on both garments and home furnishings. It is used to fasten overlapping openings and consists of two strips, one covered with tiny hooks and the other with soft loops. When the strips are pressed together, the hooks engage in the loops.

The strips can be peeled apart quickly so this type of fastening is useful for items such as children's garments, detachable collars, cuffs, trimmings and cushion covers. Touch and close fastening comes in different widths from 1.5cm to 3cm (⁵⁄₈ to 1¼in), and in various colours. 2cm (¾in) discs are also available and they can be used instead of press studs.

① Cut the fastening strip to the required length and separate the two strips.

② Place one piece in position and attach by hand or machine, stitching around the edge. Repeat for the second piece.

PRESS STUD TAPE

This type of fastening consists of press studs attached at regular intervals to a length of strong cotton tape. It is used mainly on home furnishings, especially duvet and cushion covers. The tape should be machine stitched to the fabric so that it is attached firmly enough. A piping or zip foot should be used, as an ordinary foot is too wide to fit between the edge of the tape and the studs.

① Cut the required length of tape, allowing 2cm (¾in) surplus at each end. Make sure that the first and last studs are an even distance from the ends of the opening.

② Pin the tape in position, turning under the surplus at each end. Machine stitch along each side and across the ends.

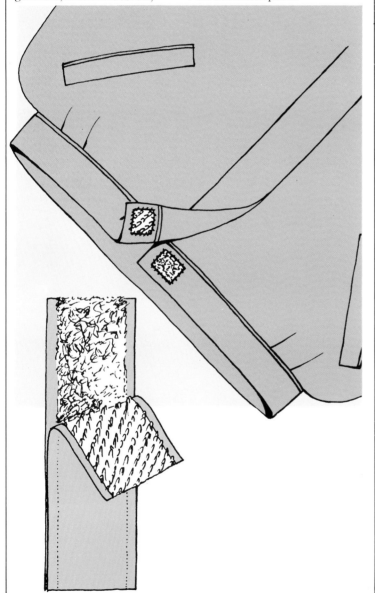

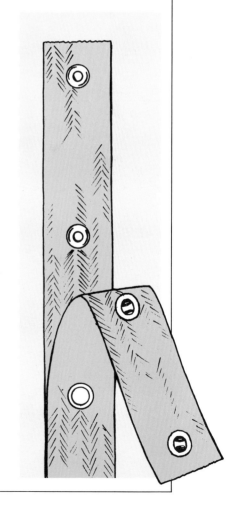

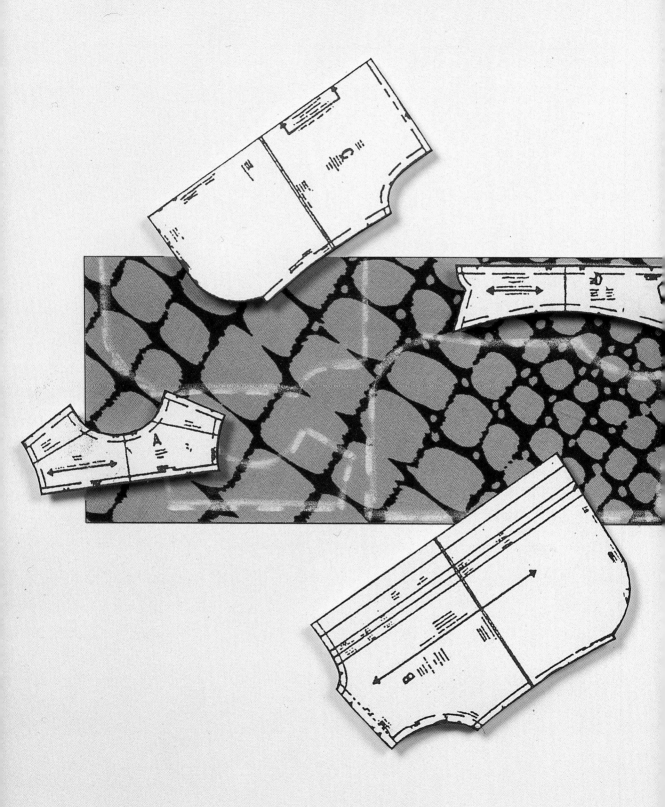

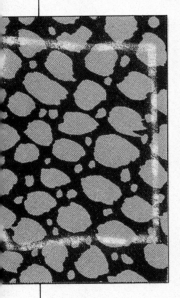

Many people prefer to make garments for both themselves and their family rather than buying them ready made. The garments are personal, less expensive, have a better fit, and there is an extensive range of fabrics and colours to choose from. This chapter takes you through the intricacies of paper patterns, and gives detailed instructions on making collars, pockets, sleeves, cuffs and waistbands.

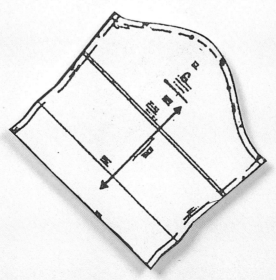

USING PAPER PATTERNS

Paper patterns for garments are produced by a number of companies and you may find that certain brands are better suited to your figure than others. You should take approximately the same size in a pattern as in a ready-made garment. If your measurements are slightly different from those on the size charts, buy a dress, blouse or jacket pattern in the size nearest to your bust measurement. It is easier to alter the waist and hips of a garment than the bust, and it is important that the pattern fits well around the shoulders and armholes. Skirt and trouser patterns are bought according to hip size. Some patterns contain several sizes and these are called multi-size patterns. Most patterns offer several variations of a garment, perhaps with different sleeves, skirt lengths or collars. Each of these variations is known as a view and the fabric requirements may be different. Paper patterns are available in different sizes and they are also arranged into several categories:

SIZE CHARTS

① **Misses'** – to fit heights between 1.65m and 1.68m (5ft 5in and 5ft 6in) and designed for a well-proportioned figure.

② **Men's** – to fit men of average build and height about 1.78m (5ft 10in) without shoes.

①

Size	6		8		10		12		14		16	
	cm	in	cm	in	cm	in	cm	in	cm	in	cm	in
Bust	78	30½	80	31½	83	32½	87	34	92	36	97	38
Waist	58	23	61	24	64	25	67	26½	71	28	76	30
Hip	83	32½	85	33½	88	34½	92	36	97	38	102	40
Back waist length	39.5	15½	40	15½	40.5	16	41.5	16¼	42	16½	42.5	16

②

Size	34		36		38		40		42		44	
	cm	in	cm	in	cm	in	cm	in	cm	in	cm	in
Chest	87	34	92	36	97	38	102	40	107	42	112	44
Waist	71	28	76	30	81	32	87	34	92	36	99	39
Hip (seat)	89	35	94	37	99	39	104	41	109	43	114	45
Neck band	33.5	14	37	14½	38	15	39.5	15½	40.5	16	42	16½
Shirt sleeve	81	32	81	32	84	33	84	33	87	34	87	34

SIZE CHARTS

③ **Half-size** – to fit heights between 1.57m and 1.6m (5ft 2in and 5ft 3in) with a well developed figure. The waist and hips are larger in proportion to the bust size in these patterns.

④ **Women's** – to fit the same height as Misses' patterns, but designed for a larger, more developed figure.

⑤ **Junior petite** – to fit an adolescent figure with a height of 1.52m (5ft) and a small bust and short back length. Patterns are also available for girls, boys, young children and toddlers.

③

Size	10½		12½		14½		16½		18½		20½	
	cm	in	cm	in	cm	in	cm	in	cm	in	cm	in
Bust	84	33	89	35	94	37	99	39	104	41	109	43
Waist	69	27	74	29	79	31	84	33	89	35	96	37½
Hip	89	35	94	37	99	39	104	41	109	43	116	45½
Back waist length	38	15	39	15¼	39.5	15½	40	15¾	40.5	15⅞	40.5	16

④

Size	38		40		42		44		46		48	
	cm	in	cm	in	cm	in	cm	in	cm	in	cm	in
Bust	107	42	112	44	117	46	122	48	127	50	132	52
Waist	89	35	94	37	99	39	105	41½	112	44	118	46½
Hip	112	44	117	46	122	48	127	50	132	52	137	54
Back waist length	44	17¼	44	17¾	44.5	17½	45	17¾	45	17¾	45.5	17⅞

⑤

Size	3jp		5jp		7jp		9jp		11jp		13jp	
	cm	in	cm	in	cm	in	cm	in	cm	in	cm	in
Bust	78	30½	79	31	81	32	84	33	87	34	89	35
Waist	57	22½	58	23	61	24	64	25	66	26	69	27
Hip	80	31½	81	32	84	33	87	34	89	35	92	36
Back waist length	35.5	14	36	14¼	37	14½	37.5	14¾	38	15	39	15¼

T A K I N G   M E A S U R E M E N T S

Personal measurements should be taken before you buy or alter a pattern. Get a friend to measure you if you can as this will be easier and much more accurate. Take all the vertical measurements indicated in the diagram first, and then the horizontal ones, keeping the tape measure taut and parallel to the ground. Write down the measurements carefully and keep them safe for future reference.

BODY AND SKIRT MEASUREMENTS

- Point of bust (shoulder to bust curve)
- Chest front (armhole to armhole)
- Bust (all around body)
- Neck to waist (front)
- Waist (front)
- Waist to hem (front)
- Side waist to hem

- Shoulder to waist (front)
- Skirt yoke (front)
- Hip (front)

- Inside arm
- Shoulder
- Shoulder to waist (back)
- Nape of neck to waist (back)
- Elbow to wrist
- Back (armhole to armhole)
- Shoulder to elbow

- Waist (back)
- Upper arm
- Skirt yoke (back)
- Hip (back)

- Wrist
- Elbow
- Waist seam (back)

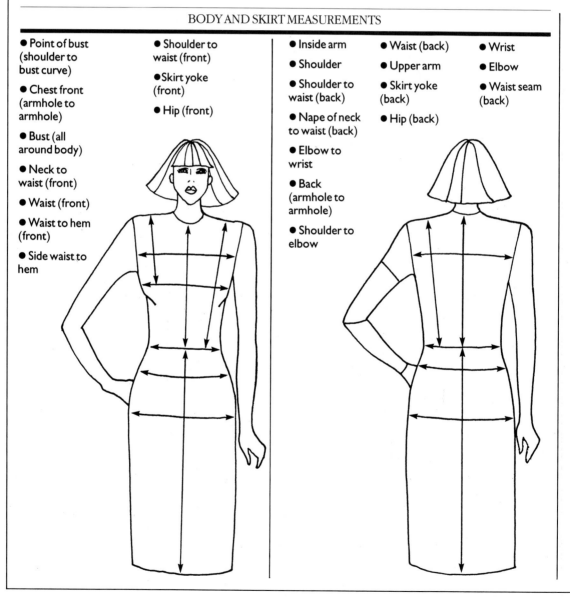

LEG MEASUREMENTS

Take waist and hip measurements (see left). Measure your inside leg from the inside top of the leg to the required height from the floor. Take your outside leg from the side waistline to the required height from the floor.

- Waist

- Hip

- Inside leg

- Outside leg

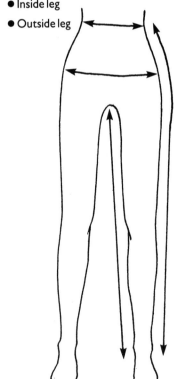

SEAT MEASUREMENTS

Sit on a chair with your back straight and measure from the side of your waist to the chair. Add $\frac{5}{8}$in. (1.5cm) for ease but for a full figure you will need to add more.

- Waist

- Depth of crotch

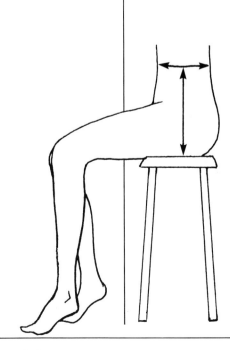

THE PATTERN ENVELOPE

UNDERSTANDING THE PATTERN ENVELOPE

When you have bought your pattern, read the information on the back of the envelope. The most important information is in the metreage (yardage) column as this tells you how much fabric to buy. Draw a ring round your size on the top row and choose the garment view and fabric width from the left-hand column. Run your finger along this line to the right until it is under your circled size. This is the amount of fabric to buy.

There may also be a back view of the garment to show the style details, and a pattern piece

diagram showing the shape of each piece and indicating which are needed for each view. At the bottom of the envelope are the measurements of the finished garment, and a list of suitable types of fabric and sewing notions such as zips and buttons.

ALTERING PATTERN PIECES

Spread the pattern sheets out flat and cut out all the pieces you will need for the garment. Cut exactly on the printed outlines; on a multi-size pattern follow the appropriate line for your size. Iron the pieces with a cool iron so that they are flat and easy to work with. Check all the measurements on the pattern pieces against your personal ones, measuring from inside the seam allowance if this is marked on the pattern; remember to allow for ease and style fullness. It is important to check the length of the pattern pieces, as this will make a difference to the fit of the garment. The pattern pieces will be marked with an adjustment or lengthening/shortening line. If an adjustment of more than 2.5cm (1in) is needed, make two smaller parallel adjustments rather than one large one.

LENGTHENING

To lengthen a pattern piece, lay it over a piece of paper and cut the pattern along the printed adjustment line. Separate the pieces until the distance between the cut edges is the same as the extra length to be inserted. Pin the pattern to the paper, keeping the cut edges of the pattern pieces parallel. Check the measurement and replace the pins with adhesive tape. Trim away the excess paper carefully, following the shape of the pattern piece.

SHORTENING

To shorten a pattern piece, fold it along the adjustment line. Make a pleat to take up the length you want to remove; remember that the folded pleat is only half the width of the unfolded pleat. Pin the pleat in place and check the length. Replace the pins with adhesive tape and trim the pattern edges so that they are even.

Other alterations to the pattern pieces are made in a similar way, by adding extra paper or by pleating the pattern to remove length or width.

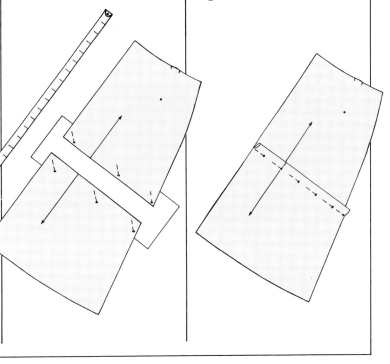

C O N S T R U C T I O N   M A R K S

Each pattern piece has a series of construction marks printed on it. Most of the marks will be transferred to the fabric before the pattern is removed and used as a guide when sewing. You should make yourself familiar with the marks.

CONSTRUCTION MARKS

Stitching line This is a broken line 1.5cm (⅝in) from the cutting line which indicates that there is a seam allowance of 1.5cm (⅝in) included on the pattern; you will stitch along this line. If no stitching line is indicated, the seam allowance may need to be added by cutting out fabric 1.5cm (⅝in) larger than the pattern piece. Always check whether the seam allowance is included. Most multi-size patterns will not have cutting lines though seam allowances are usually included.

Cutting line This is the continuous line on the outer edge of the pattern piece and you should follow this line accurately when cutting out the fabric. On a multi-size pattern, there will be several cutting lines with each one corresponding to a particular size.

Fold line This is represented by a line with arrows at right angles at either end, pointing to the edge of the pattern. This edge is placed on a fold of fabric so that the piece unfolds to a single whole piece after cutting out.

Grain line This is a line with arrows at either end and it should be placed parallel to the selvedge so that it is on the true straight grain of the fabric.

Easing line This is represented by a row of short broken lines with an arrow and dot at each end. It indicates a section of fabric, usually on a curve, which will need to be eased gently in order to fit the piece it is being joined to.

Dart marks The positions of the darts are indicated by broken lines which meet at a point.

Gathering line This is indicated by two rows of short broken lines with arrows at each end. Dots mark the points at each end of the rows of gathering stitches.

Buttonholes The position of the buttonholes is marked by a circle or dot with a horizontal line.

Adjustment line This is a double line, indicating where a pattern can be shortened or lengthened.

Balance marks These are usually represented by either single or double notches and are used to match one piece of fabric to another. Dots, squares and triangles are sometimes used instead of notches.

Zip position This is indicated by a dot or notch at the base of the opening; or by a line of small triangles showing the exact position of the zip.

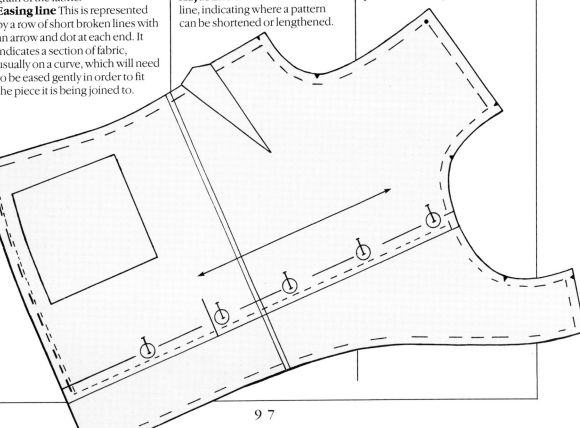

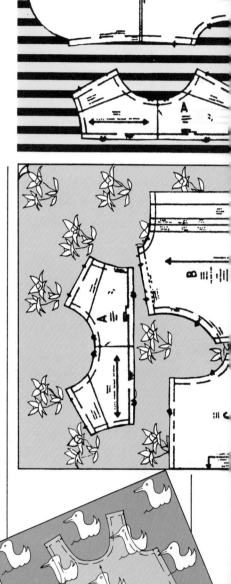

PREPARING THE FABRIC

Even-weave fabric should have the warp and weft threads lying at right angles to each other. If they do not, the fabric is off-grain and will not hang properly when the garment is finished.

To check the straightness of the grain, cut through the selvedge at one edge of the fabric. Pull one of the weft threads which run across to the other selvedge. Pull this

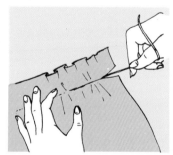

thread gently, gathering up the fabric, and cut along the pulled thread as far as you can. Repeat the pulling and cutting sequence until you reach the other selvedge. Fold the fabric in half lengthwise and check if the cut edge is level. If the cut edge does not meet correctly, you will then need to straighten the grain.

To straighten the grain, pin the cut edges and the selvedges. Wrinkles will form on the fabric. Press the fabric along the lengthwise grain with a steam iron, avoiding the fold, and pressing out the wrinkles. If necessary, repeat this along the crosswise grain.

LAYING OUT THE PATTERN

Assemble all the equipment that you need for cutting and lay out the fabric on a clean, flat surface. A guide will be included with the pattern pieces to show you how to lay them out on different widths of fabric. These layouts will differ for fabrics with a nap or one-way design. Check that you have all the pieces you will need before you begin to lay them out. Lay out the pieces according to the layout diagram, paying particular attention to pieces such as sleeves, pockets and facings, which may need to be cut out twice. Make sure that the pieces that need to lie on a fold do so.

You will need to alter the suggested layout if the fabric you are using has a large pattern, and you should buy a little extra fabric to allow for this. Large pattern motifs should be centred on the front and back of a garment, and also on each sleeve. Always try to cut a collar so that the pattern matches from point to point.

Fabrics with a nap or one-way design should have the pattern pieces laid out in the same direction and this will require extra fabric if the pattern does not include a nap layout. The diagram shows a layout for a fabric with a one-way design.

Checks and stripes should match at the side and centre seams, waistlines, armholes and sleeves, and it is a good idea to choose a pattern without too

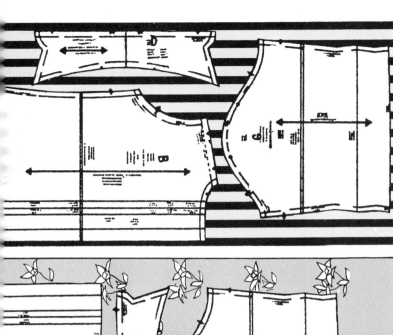

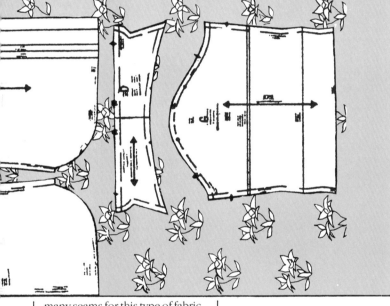

many seams for this type of fabric. Move the pattern pieces so that corresponding notches line up on the same check or stripe. Take care to match the checks or stripes on the actual stitching line, rather than on the cutting line.

When you are sure that the pieces are laid out correctly, pin them to the fabric. Place the pins diagonally just inside the seam lines to prevent the fabric from puckering. Cut out the pieces along the cutting line, cutting the main pieces first. Transfer the construction marks to the fabric using tailor's tacks before unpinning the pattern.

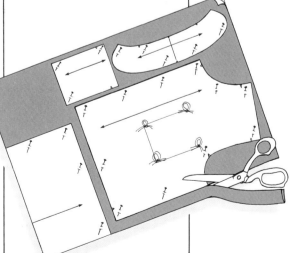

ORDER OF MAKING UP

Making up a garment is a fairly straightforward process if it is done in a logical sequence. For example, if you are making a dress with a waistline seam, make the bodice and skirt up separately and then join them together. The instructions supplied with your pattern will tell you the correct sequence for the particular garment you are making, and they should be followed meticulously, step by step. However, there are a few rules to bear in mind.

● Each section of the garment— bodice, skirt, sleeves, cuffs, collar and pockets — should be made up first and then joined to the others to form the complete garment.

● Always tack the main seams and darts by hand and make any fitting alterations before machine stitching. This will prevent your having to unpick the machine stitches which can leave a permanent mark. Transfer any alterations to the paper pattern in case you wish to make up the garment again.

● Test the stitch tension and length first on a spare piece of fabric.

● Neaten the seams as you go along and press each seam and dart as it is completed.

● When pressing, put the iron on the fabric along the grain, never across the grain. Do not use undue pressure or the fabric could stretch out of shape. Use a pressing cloth on all fabrics except cotton and linen and press on the wrong side of the fabric to avoid shine. Take great care when pressing bulky areas and do not press over pins. Press using a sleeve board and a tailor's ham in the appropriate areas.

FITTING GARMENTS

Once the main seams and darts have been tacked, pin the other seams together. Try on the garment, wearing the underwear and shoes that you intend to wear with it when it is finished. Try it on right side out and pin any openings together. Put on a belt if there is to be one, and check the fit of the garment in front of a full length mirror.

The garment should feel comfortable when you sit down, stretch and bend. Any excess fabric will need to be taken into the appropriate seam or dart, or some seams may have to be let out slightly. If any adjustments have to be made, remove the tacking stitches and pin the alterations before trying on the garment again. When you are satisfied with the fit, tack the seams and begin stitching.

Follow this check list when you try on a garment:

● The shoulder seam should be on top of the shoulder and not slope to the front or to the back. If this happens, you will have to adjust the seam slightly.

● Bust darts should point to the fullest part of the bust. Sleeve darts should point to the elbow. Adjust the darts if necessary.

● Necklines should fit snugly without gaping. A badly fitting neckline can be corrected by taking in the centre back and shoulder seams or by making tiny darts at the back of the neck.

● Side, back and front seams should run in a straight, vertical line.

● The waistline seam should be in the correct position.

An interfacing is an extra layer of fabric placed between layers of the garment fabric. It adds body and permanent shape to the garment as well as reinforcing the fabric. The type of interfacing to use will depend both on the type of garment and the fabric from which it is made. Interfacing should never be heavier in weight than the garment fabric.

Interfacing comes in various weights and degrees of firmness; some types may be sewn in and others are ironed on to the fabric. Your paper pattern will tell you which garment pieces will need interfacing. The chart shows suitable types of interfacing for garments and fabrics.

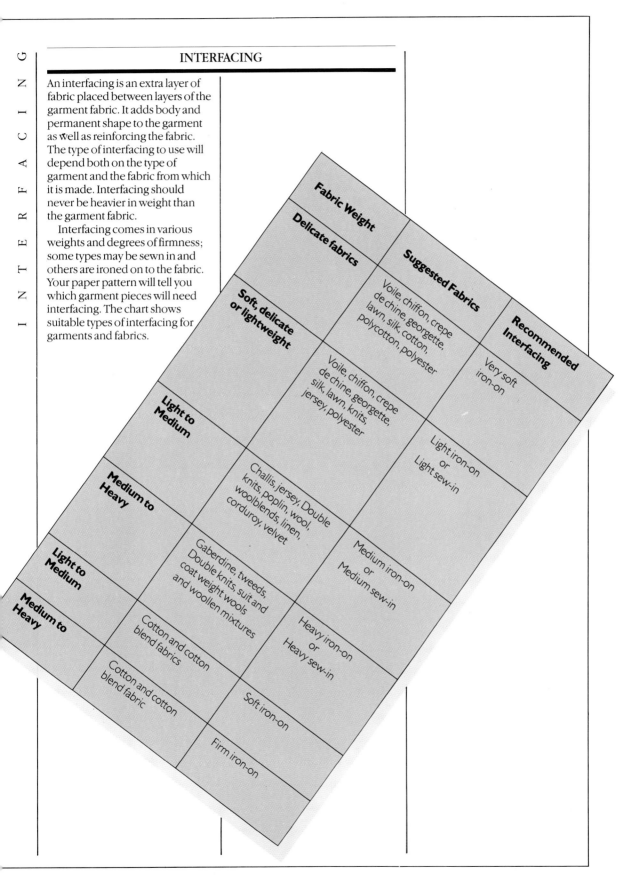

Fabric Weight	Suggested Fabrics	Recommended Interfacing
Delicate fabrics		
Soft, delicate or lightweight	Voile, chiffon, crepe de chine, georgette, lawn, silk, cotton, polycotton, polyester	Very soft iron-on
Light to Medium	Voile, chiffon, crepe de chine, georgette, silk, lawn, knits, jersey, polyester	Light iron-on or Light sew-in
Medium to Heavy	Challis, jersey, Double knits, poplin, wool, woolblends, linen, corduroy, velvet	Medium iron-on or Medium sew-in
Light to Medium	Gaberdine, tweeds, Double knits, suit and coat weight wools and woollen mixtures	Heavy iron-on or Heavy sew-in
Medium to Heavy	Cotton and cotton blend fabrics	Soft iron-on
	Cotton and cotton blend fabric	Firm iron-on

L I N I N G

Lining a garment will help to prolong its life as it prevents the fabric from becoming baggy and pulling out of shape. Lining also neatens the inside by covering the seam edges – essential on a jacket or coat. A lining will also make an outer garment more comfortable to wear, as it will prevent the fabric from sticking to the garments underneath.

A loose lining, which is made separately from the garment and attached later, is the easiest type to make. The lining should be the same size as the garment and made without stitching details such as darts. It should fit without pulling or straining. Fabrics for lining should be slippery and quite soft. The most commonly used materials are fine man-made fabrics and inexpensive silks.

On lined skirts and dresses, the hem of the lining is finished separately from the garment hem.

LINING

① Finish the hem of the garment in the appropriate way. Turn the garment inside out and fold back the excess lining at the hem, so that the fold of the lining hem is 2.5cm (1in) from the hemline of the garment. Trim away any surplus lining from the hem.

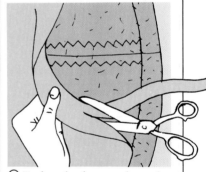

② Tuck under the raw edge and pin and tack the lining hem in place. Take care not to catch the fabric hem in the stitches. Machine stitch around the hem to provide a durable finish.

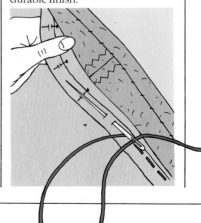

LINING

③ Secure the lining to the garment at the side seams by making three or four long stitches, as shown. Reinforce the stitches by working over them with blanket stitch.

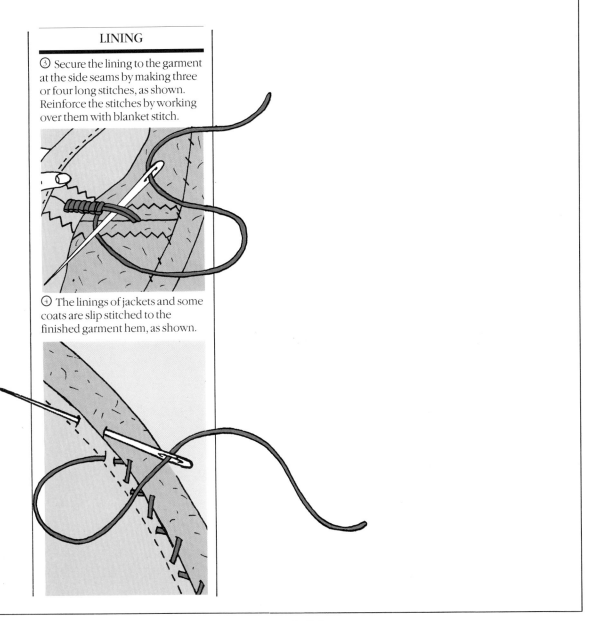

④ The linings of jackets and some coats are slip stitched to the finished garment hem, as shown.

Necklines are finished by adding a collar, by binding the raw edge with a bias strip or by attaching a matching piece of fabric called a facing. Armholes on sleeveless garments are also finished with a facing or a binding. The bodice darts and shoulder seams should be finished and the zip inserted before the facing is added. Interfacing can be added to the facing pieces before stitching to give the neckline a firmer finish.

FACING A ROUND NECK

① Join the facing at the shoulder seams and neaten the seams. Press the seams open. Neaten the edge of the facing that will not be attached to the garment by turning 5mm (¼in) to the wrong side and stitching it in place.
② Pin the facing to the garment with the right sides together, matching the shoulder seams and notches. Tack and stitch it in place.
③ Trim the facing seam allowance to 3mm (⅛in) and the garment seam allowance to 5mm (¼in). Clip the curves and trim away excess fabric where the seams cross the stitched line. Press the seam.

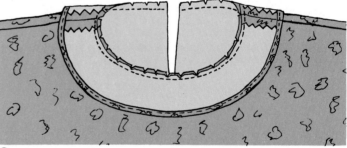

④ Pull the facing to the outside of the neckline. Stitch around the neckline through both the facing and the seam allowances. Stitch as close to the seamline as possible and press the stitching.
⑤ Turn the facing to the inside so that the seamline lies inside the neckline. Tack the facing in place and press it well.
⑥ Slip stitch the facing to the garment at the shoulder seams. Fold in the edges along the seamline at the ends of the facing and slip stitch them in place along the zip.

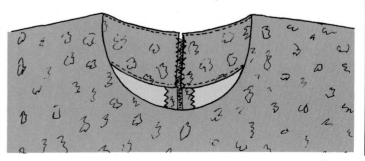

FACING A SQUARE NECK

Follow the instructions for facing a round neck, but pivot the fabric when stitching the corners, and clip the corners to within 3mm (1/8in) of the seamline.

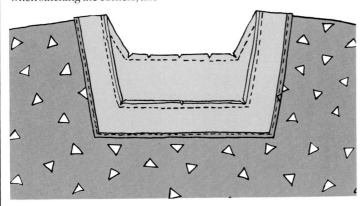

FACING A 'V' NECK

Follow the instructions for facing a round neck, but pivot the fabric at the point of the 'V' and clip the edges as shown.

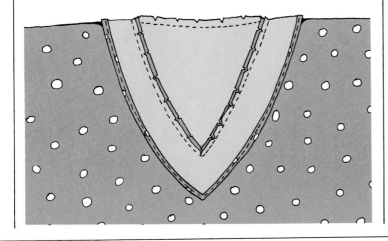

COLLARS

Styles of collar vary, but the methods for attaching them to a garment are virtually the same. The neckline of the garment and the neck edge of the collar must match perfectly in order to give a good fit. All matching notches should line up and the collar seam allowances should be trimmed to minimize bulk.

TWO PIECE COLLAR

STAND COLLAR

MAKING A TWO-PIECE COLLAR

This type of collar consists of an upper and under collar and an interfacing.

① Pin and tack the interfacing to the wrong side of the upper collar. If you are using iron-on interfacing, press it on to the wrong side of the upper collar following the manufacturer's instructions.

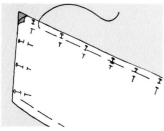

② Place the upper collar and the under collar together with the right sides facing. Pin and tack around the outer edge, leaving the neck edge open.

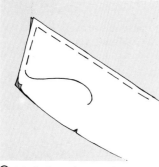

③ Stitch along the seamline around the outer edge. Trim the interfacing close to the stitched line. Trim the under collar seam allowance to 3mm (1/8in), and the upper collar allowance to 5mm (1/4in). Clip any curves almost to the line of stitching.

④ Press the stitching. On a round collar, turn the collar to the right side and tack near the edge to hold the layers in place. Press the collar.

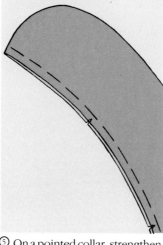

⑤ On a pointed collar, strengthen the corners with a few smaller stitches and trim the seam allowances across the points. Turn it to the right side and gently push the points out with a bodkin or fine knitting needle. Tack and press as above.

⑥ Attach a two-piece collar by the second method described.

MAKING A STAND COLLAR

This type of collar is close fitting and stands up around the neckline. It can have an opening at the front or at the back. It is cut on the bias and must be interfaced.

① Apply the interfacing to the wrong side of the outer collar. Pin the outer and inner collars together with the right sides facing and tack together, leaving the neck edge open.

② Stick along the seamline. Trim the interfacing close to the stitched line and the seam allowances down to 5mm (1/4in). Cut across the corners close to the stitched line to minimize bulk, and clip the curved edge.

③ Turn the collar to the right side. Pin and tack along the edge and press well. Attach the collar to the garment using the second method.

MAKING A ROLL COLLAR

A roll collar is made from one piece of fabric cut on the bias and folded in half before stitching. It is folded again when it is worn to give a soft neckline. This type of collar does not need interfacing and it can be attached by either of the methods described.

① Fold the collar in half with the right sides facing and matching the notches. Tack along each end.

② Stitch the ends, leaving the neck edge open. Trim the seam allowance of the inner half of the collar to 3mm (1/8in) and that of the outer to 6mm (1/4in). Cut across the corners.

③ Turn the collar to the right side and push out the corners gently. Press the seams but avoid pressing the fold.

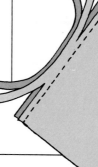

MAKING A SHIRT COLLAR WITH A STAND

This collar consists of a two-piece collar which is mounted on a stand collar to give it height.

① Make up the two-piece collar as described above. Interface the wrong side of the outer stand.

② Insert the made up collar between the two pieces of the stand with the right sides facing and the notches matching. Pin and tack through all the layers and then stitch along the seamline.

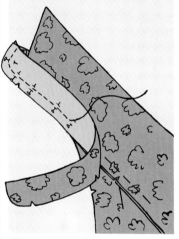

③ Trim the interfacings and the seam allowances and grade them to eliminate bulk.

④ Turn the stand to the right side and press it. Attach it to the garment by the first method described.

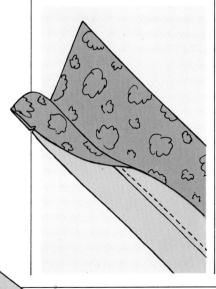

ATTACHING A COLLAR WITHOUT A FACING

If the garment has an opening, it should be finished before the collar is attached.

① Place the under collar on the neckline of the garment with the right sides together and matching the notches. Pin the under collar to the garment.

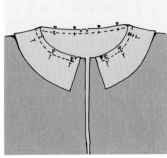

② Stitch along the seamline and trim the seam allowances to 5mm (¼in). Fold the collar up and tuck the trimmed seam allowance into the collar. Press it in place.

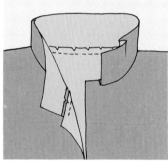

③ Turn under the seam allowance on the upper collar. Pin and tack it in position as shown. Slip stitch it to the garment along the seam line.

ATTACHING A COLLAR WITH A FACING

If a collar is made in two pieces without a stand this method of attachment is best.

① Place the collar on the garment neckline with the under collar to the right side of the garment. Lay the facing over it with the right sides facing and matching the notches.

② Pin the layers together and tack in place. Stitch along the seamline of the facing. Trim the seam allowances and corners and clip the curve of the neckline almost up to the stitched line.

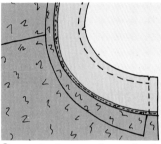

③ Fold the facing to the inside of the garment and push out the corners. Tack the facing in place and press it well.

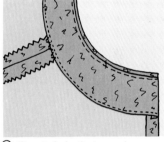

④ Slip stitch the facing to the garment where it crosses the seams.

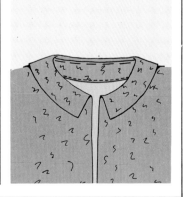

There are several different styles of sleeve but they are all based on one of the following three types.

SET-IN SLEEVE

This is the most common type of sleeve and it is cut separately from the garment and inserted into the armhole. The length and width of the sleeve can differ, but the method of insertion is the same. Finish seams and the lower edge of the sleeve as desired before inserting it.

① Work two rows of gathering stitches between the notches at the head of the sleeve. Turn the sleeve to the right side and position it in the armhole, with the right sides of the fabric facing.

② Pin at the underarm, shoulder seam and notches, working from the inside of the sleeve and setting the pins at right angles to the edge of the fabric. Gather up the fullness at both sides of the sleeve towards the shoulder line until it fits the armhole exactly.

③ Spread the gathers evenly and pin this section of the sleeve to the armhole. Tack and stitch the sleeve in place, starting at the underarm seam.

④ Remove the gathering stitches and trim the seam allowances down slightly. Neaten the raw edges and press the seam.

RAGLAN SLEEVE

A raglan sleeve is attached to the back and front of the garment with a long diagonal seam running underneath the arm.

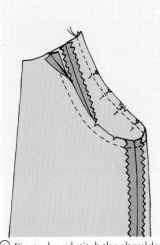

① Pin, tack and stitch the shoulder dart if the sleeve is cut in one piece. Slash the dart and finish the edges as appropriate. For a two-piece sleeve, pin, tack and stitch the shoulder seam and neaten the edges.

② Pin, tack and stitch the underarm seam of the sleeve and the side seam of the garment. Neaten the edges and press the seams open.

③ Turn the sleeve to the right side and pin it to the garment with the right sides facing and matching the notches. Tack and stitch in a continuous line from one neck edge to the other. Remove the tacking stitches.

④ Clip and notch the seams along the curves so that they will lie flat. Neaten the edges and press the seams to one side.

KIMONO SLEEVE

Kimono sleeves are usually cut in one piece with the body of the garment.

① With the right sides of the garment facing, pin, tack and stitch the side and underarm seams together. Shorten the stitch length on the curve to make the seam stronger.

② Clip the curves at intervals and finish the raw edges. Press the seams open. On the wrong side of the garment, tack a 15cm (5½in) length of straight seam binding along the curve of the underarm seam.

③ On the right side of the garment, work two parallel lines of stitching each 3mm (⅛in) from the seamline. Pull the thread ends through to the wrong side and fasten them off.

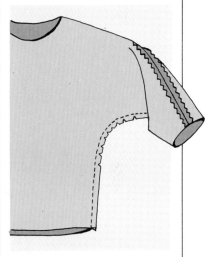

S L E E V E   O P E N I N G S

If you intend to add a cuff, you will have to make an opening in the sleeve to allow your hand to go through easily. The opening should be finished before the cuff is attached. Sleeve openings are on the side of the sleeve towards the back. They can be finished with either a facing or a narrow binding.

FACED OPENING

① Cut a strip of matching fabric 3cm (1¼in) longer than the opening and 7cm (2¾in) wide. Neaten the two long sides and one short one by turning 5mm (¼in) of the fabric to the wrong side and stitching in place. With the right sides facing, tack the strip over the opening with the centre of the strip over the cutting line on the sleeve.

② Stitch round the opening 5mm (¼in) from the cutting line, as shown, curving the stitching at the top of the opening. Cut to the top of the stitching.

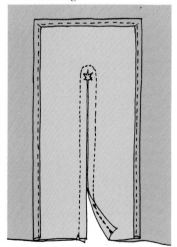

③ Turn the facing to the wrong side of the sleeve and tack it in place. Press the opening and slip stitch the facing to the sleeve. Do not remove the tacking stitches until the cuff has been attached.

BOUND OPENING

① Cut the opening to within 5mm (¼in) of the top. Cut a bias strip of fabric twice as long as the opening plus 2cm (¾in). The strip should be about 3.5cm (1⅜in) wide.

② With the right sides facing, position one edge of the strip along the left-hand edge of the opening. Stitch along this side and then curve the strip at the top of the opening and stitch around the curve. Continue stitching along the right-hand side.

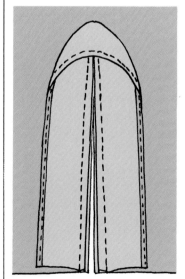

③ Reinforce the curve with a short row of smaller stitches and then finish the binding in the usual way.

The lower edge of the sleeve can be finished in various ways. A simple hem is neat on a short or three-quarter length sleeve, while fuller sleeves can be finished with a cuff.

MAKING A WRAP-OVER CUFF

This cuff is used on dresses, blouses and shirts and is cut from a straight piece of fabric. It wraps over at the opening and is fastened by buttons.
① Apply the interfacing to the wrong side of the cuff. Fold the cuff in half lengthways with the right sides facing. Tack the ends and stitch along the seamline.

② Trim the interfacing close to the stitching. Trim the seam allowance on the inner half of the cuff to 3mm (⅛in) and that on the outer half of the cuff to 5mm (¼in). Cut the corners close to the stitching.
③ Press and turn the cuff to the right side. Push out the corners so that they are sharp and press again.

ATTACHING A BASIC CUFF

Finish the sleeve seam, check the length of the sleeve and finish the opening before attaching the cuff.
① Work two rows of gathering stitches around the bottom of the sleeve. Pull up the stitches until the sleeve fits the cuff.
② With the right sides facing, pin the interfaced half of the cuff to the sleeve, working from the sleeve side.
③ Match the notches and arrange the gathers evenly. Tack and stitch the cuff to the sleeve. Trim the seam allowances to 5mm (¼in).
④ Turn the cuff away from the sleeve and press the seam towards the cuff. Fold the free edge of the cuff along the seamline and slip stitch it to the machine-stitched line. Press the cuff and remove the tacking stitches.

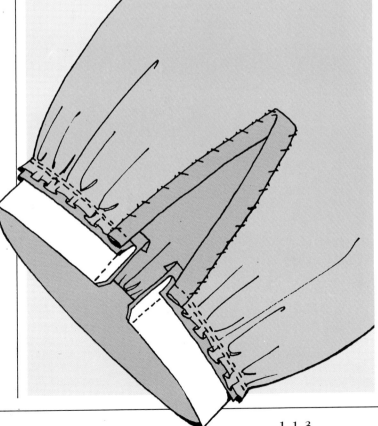

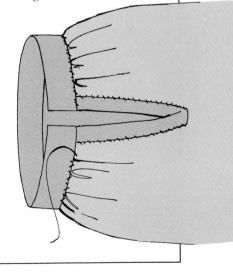

P O C K E T S

Pockets can be functional or purely decorative. They should always be firmly attached to the garment. Pockets can be made separately and added to the garment, or they can be concealed in the garment seam.

PATCH POCKET

A patch pocket is stitched on to a garment; it can have rounded or square corners at the base.
① Apply soft interfacing to the wrong side of the outer pocket. Fold the pocket in half with the right sides together and pin. Tack and stitch along the seamline, leaving an opening in the centre of the lower edge for turning the pocket out.

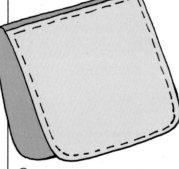

② Trim the interfacing and seam allowances as for a collar, and cut off the corners, or notch the curves. Turn the pocket to the right

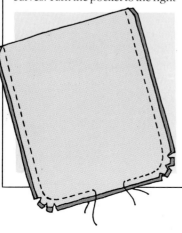

side and push out the corners. Slip stitch across the opening to close.
③ Pin and tack the pocket in position on the garment. Stitch round three sides, finishing off the stitching securely at the top corners.

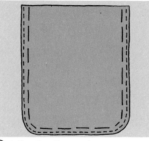

④ A flap for the pocket can be made in the same way. It should be slightly wider than the pocket, but shallower. Follow steps 1 and 2 above, and work any decorative stitching or buttonholes before attaching the flap.

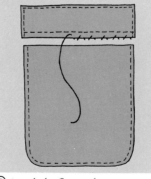

⑤ Attach the flap to the garment just above the pocket and press it downwards.

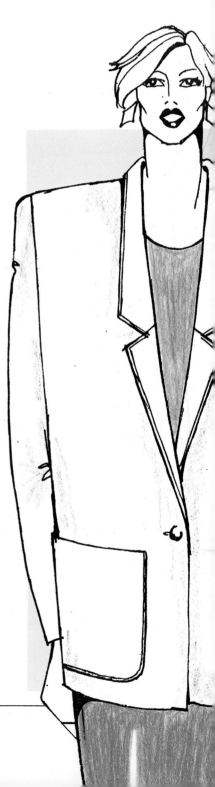

CONCEALED POCKET

A concealed pocket lies neatly in the side seam of a garment and is usually made from matching fabric.

① Place one section of the pocket with right sides facing along the seamline of the garment between the position marks. Pin and tack in place. Stitch 1cm (⅜in) from the edge between the marks and press the pocket piece away from the garment.

② Repeat step 1 for the other half of the pocket. With the right sides facing and matching the notches, place the two garment pieces together. Pin, tack and stitch along the seamline, pivoting the fabric at the corners to stitch the seam and around the pocket in one operation.

③ Press the seam, clip into the angle of the seam allowance on the back of the garment and neaten the raw edges. Press the garment seam open.

The best finish for the waistline of a skirt or pair of trousers is a waistband. It should fit snugly and be firm enough not to crease during wear. An alternative finish to a stiffened band is an elasticated one, which can also be used to finish a sleeve, providing that it is not too full. Waistbands are attached after the main part of the garment is finished, but before the hem is levelled.

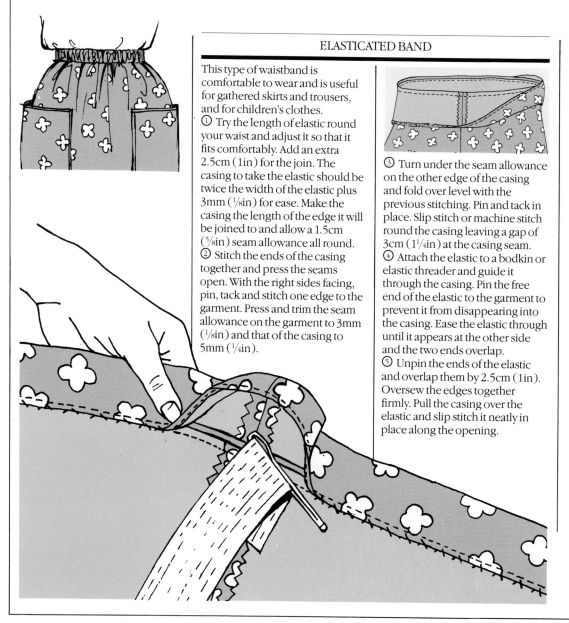

ELASTICATED BAND

This type of waistband is comfortable to wear and is useful for gathered skirts and trousers, and for children's clothes.

① Try the length of elastic round your waist and adjust it so that it fits comfortably. Add an extra 2.5cm (1in) for the join. The casing to take the elastic should be twice the width of the elastic plus 3mm (⅛in) for ease. Make the casing the length of the edge it will be joined to and allow a 1.5cm (⅝in) seam allowance all round.

② Stitch the ends of the casing together and press the seams open. With the right sides facing, pin, tack and stitch one edge to the garment. Press and trim the seam allowance on the garment to 3mm (⅛in) and that of the casing to 5mm (¼in).

③ Turn under the seam allowance on the other edge of the casing and fold over level with the previous stitching. Pin and tack in place. Slip stitch or machine stitch round the casing leaving a gap of 3cm (1¼in) at the casing seam.

④ Attach the elastic to a bodkin or elastic threader and guide it through the casing. Pin the free end of the elastic to the garment to prevent it from disappearing into the casing. Ease the elastic through until it appears at the other side and the two ends overlap.

⑤ Unpin the ends of the elastic and overlap them by 2.5cm (1in). Oversew the edges together firmly. Pull the casing over the elastic and slip stitch it neatly in place along the opening.

STIFFENED BAND

Buy special waistband stiffening for this type of waistband as interfacing is not quite stiff enough.

① Place the waistband on to the garment waist with the right sides facing, and match the notches. Pin, tack and stitch in place.

② Pin the strip of stiffening on to the band as shown, with the edge on the line of stitching. Tack it in place and stitch from the other side, close to the edge. Trim the garment seam allowance close to the stitching and the waistband allowance 3mm ($\frac{1}{8}$in) wider.

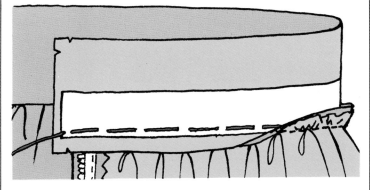

③ Fold the waistband back along the stiffening and press the seams and the band away from the skirt. Stitch the ends of the band and trim away the surplus fabric.

④ Turn the waistband right side out and turn under the seam allowance on the unstitched edge. Pin it in place and slip stitch it to the garment.

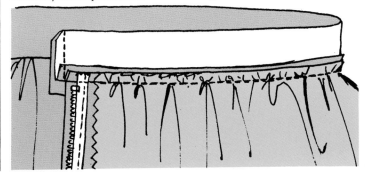

If you intend to wear a belt over a stiffened waistband, keep it in place by adding belt carriers. They can be stitched or made from strips of matching fabric.

STITCHED CARRIERS

These are less prominent than fabric carriers, but not as strong. Make them from a matching buttonhole twist thread.
① Work a double loop of thread in the right position for the belt and wide enough to accommodate it comfortably.
② Reinforce the loop by working blanket stitches along it, packing them tightly together.

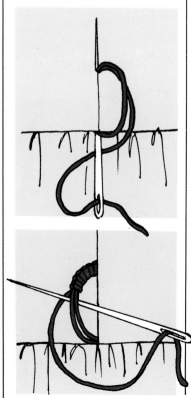

FABRIC CARRIERS

Fabric carriers are strong and should be used for a wide belt and on trousers in preference to the stitched type.
① Cut a strip of matching fabric for each carrier 3cm (1¼in) wide and long enough to take the belt, plus 3cm (1¼in) for ease and turnings. Fold the strip lengthways with the right sides together.
② Pin and stitch the strip 5mm (¼in) from the raw edge. Trim the seam allowance to 3mm (⅛in) turn to the right side and press with the seam at the centre of one side.
③ Attach each carrier by turning 5mm (¼in) of the fabric under at each end and stitching them in position with the seam concealed under the carrier.

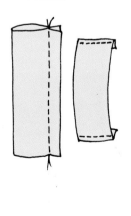

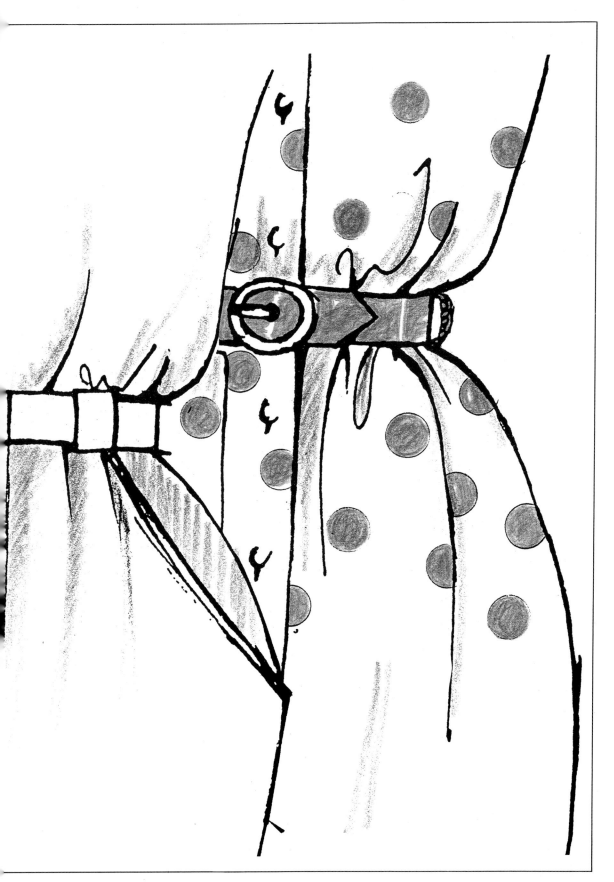

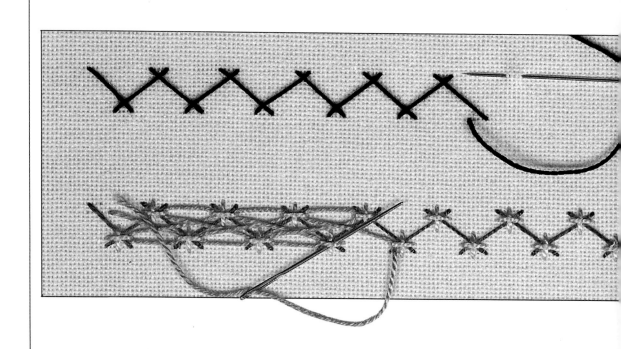

You can add a distinctive touch to your clothing and home furnishings in many different ways. Colour is important, as is the use of pattern and decoration. Style is very individual and something which pleases you visually may not please others! Probably the best way to begin developing your own style is to build on a simple, fairly neutral colour scheme. Gradually add touches of different colours to react with this.

COLOUR

There are no hard and fast rules when choosing which particular colours to put together, as they tend to interact in different ways. You may like certain combinations and hate others: you may decide to use only dark and light tones of one colour. A tonal colour scheme will give a natural continuity to an outfit or a room. Another idea is to add touches of the bright primary colours, red, blue and yellow, to a white, grey or cream basic scheme. Dark colours such as black, dark grey and navy blue can be terrific for a basic wardrobe when accessorized with hot fuchsia pink, scarlet or an acid yellow.

Reds, yellows and oranges are warm to live with, while blues and greens give the impression of being cool. Pinks and mauves can be cool or warm in appearance, depending on whether the shades tend towards blue or towards red. This could be an important consideration when choosing colours for curtains and bed-linen. For example, if you have a north-facing bedroom, it will appear colder if you use shades of blue. The same room will have a sunnier aspect if you choose a warm shade of yellow for the furnishings instead. Light tones of a cool colour will make a room look larger than it is and dark tones will make it look smaller.

PATTERN

Fabric can be plain, textured or patterned. Patterns range from tiny checks, stripes and neat, geometric designs to huge, splashy florals and abstracts. Areas of pattern on curtains or cushion covers can liven up a plain expanse of a neutral colour quite dramatically. A small, regular geometric print will provide a good foil for a stunning floral pattern, while two or three large patterns used together might cancel each other out visually. The same pattern can look very different when printed in other colourways. A pattern in bright, garish colours may appear as though it would be difficult to live with, but the same pattern could be pleasing printed in soft landscape shades of muted greens and browns.

A large pattern on clothing tends to make the wearer look bigger than a small regular one. The same is true of light colours, shiny or heavily textured fabrics, and strong horizontal stripes.

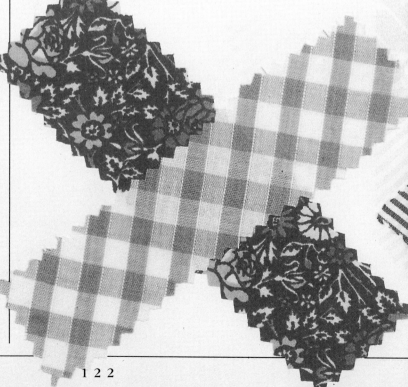

DECORATION

Fabric can be decorated simply and quickly by the addition of lace, braid, ribbon and fringing. Lace and fringing are usually added into a seam in the same way as piping, while ribbon and braid are stitched directly on to the fabric. Wide borders can be built up using multiple straight rows of ribbon, braid or machine embroidery, especially if you have a sewing machine that produces decorative patterns. These can be used to enhance simple garments, table-linen and cushion covers. Ornamental patterns can also be worked using ribbon and braid.

Other forms of decoration include hand embroidery, appliqué, applying beads and sequins, and quilting. Fabric can be its own decoration if it is pieced together as patchwork.

RIBBON AND BRAID

Ribbons and braids have been used for centuries to decorate clothes and furnishings. When working patterns make sure that neither the background fabric nor the braid puckers, and that curves and corners are neat and well finished.

① Mark the pattern on to the background fabric with tailor's chalk or a special marking pen that will wash out. Lay the braid or ribbon on top, turning under the raw edges at the ends, and tack in position.

② Corners and angles are formed by turning the braid over as shown. When working curves, tack the outer edges of each curve in place first. Gather the inner edges of the curves until they fit the marked pattern lines and then tack them in place.

③ Stitch the braid or ribbon to the fabric along each edge using back stitch or running stitch and a matching colour of thread.

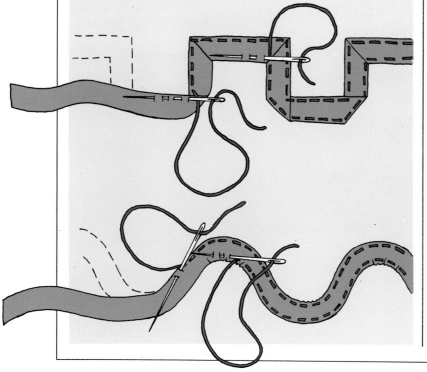

BEADS AND SEQUINS

Beads and sequins can glamorize an ordinary garment very successfully. They can be used to create single motifs or borders and, although stitching them by hand is quite a time-consuming process, the end result will be worth while.

Sequins can be applied so the stitches show on the surface or so they are concealed. If the stitches are going to show, use a pretty thread such as a twisted silk or three strands of stranded embroidery cotton.

Beads can be applied individually or couched down in a continuous line. The stitches should not show on the right side of the fabric. Some beads have only a very tiny hole, so you may need to buy special beading needles for stitching them on. Use a fine, strong thread and take care to secure the beginning and end of the thread firmly.

APPLYING SEQUINS

① To apply sequins with the stitches showing, bring the needle through to the right side of the fabric and thread it through the eye of the first sequin. Work a back stitch over the right side of the sequin and bring the needle back through the fabric at the left of the sequin, ready to thread through the next one. Continue until all the sequins are stitched on to the fabric and secure the end of the thread on the wrong side.

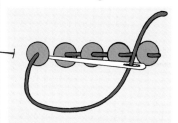

② To apply sequins with invisible stitches, work a back stitch over the left side of the first sequin. Place the next sequin so that it overlaps the first one and bring the needle through the fabric at the left-hand edge of the sequin. Work a back stitch from the edge of the sequin, taking the needle through the eye and inserting it into the hole of the previous back stitch. Repeat this sequence until all the sequins are in place and secure the thread on the wrong side.

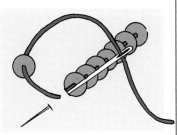

APPLYING BEADS

① To stitch beads individually, bring the needle through the fabric and thread the bead on to it. Insert the needle into the fabric through the same hole and bring it back through the fabric where you want the next bead to be placed.

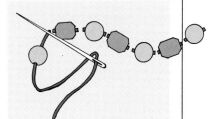

② To stitch beads in a continuous line, cut two lengths of thread. Bring one thread through to the right side of the fabric and thread the beads on to it. Slide the first bead into position and, using the second thread, work a small stitch close to the bead and over the first thread, as shown. Slide the next bead into position and repeat the process. Continue in this way until all the beads have been couched on to the fabric.

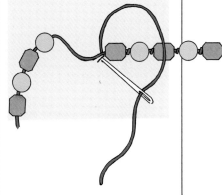

HAND EMBROIDERY

Hand embroidery has been used for centuries to embellish garments and home furnishings, and it can be as simple or ornate as you like. Add embroidered motifs and monograms to your clothes, borders to table-linen and work larger pieces to make into stunning cushion covers. If you are new to embroidery, practise the stitches first on some spare fabric until you feel confident using them. As with most skills, practice makes perfect, so do not be discouraged by your first attempts if they do not seem very professional.

Details are given in this section of the threads and needles used for embroidery, and instructions are provided for transferring a design to your fabric. A selection of stitches is shown in easy-to-work steps.

EMBROIDERY HOOP

All embroidery will be more successful if the fabric is held taut in an embroidery hoop. It is not only easier to handle, but the stitches will be more regular and distortion of the fabric will be kept to a minimum. If the area of embroidery is quite large, the hoop can be easily moved along the fabric after a portion of the stitching has been completed.

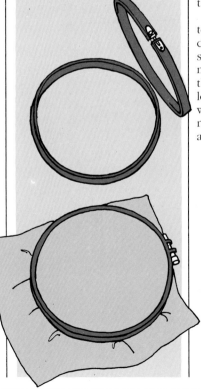

NEEDLES

Crewel and chenille needles are used for embroidery on fabric. They have larger eyes than ordinary sewing needles to accommodate a thicker thread. Crewel needles are of medium length and are used for fine and medium-weight embroidery. Chenille needles are longer and thicker, and have larger eyes than crewel needles, which makes them suitable for use with heavier threads and fabrics.

All needles are graded from fine to thick, with the lower number denoting the thicker needle. The size of needle to use is really a matter of personal preference, but the eye should be large enough to let the thread pass through it without fraying. Always use a fine needle if you are embroidering on a light, delicate fabric.

THREADS

Embroidery threads are available in a wide range of weights and colours. The most common threads are made from cotton and wool, but pure silk, linen, synthetic and metallic threads can also be bought. Some threads are tightly twisted and cannot be divided, while others are made up of several strands which can be separated to give a finer thread. The strands can be put together to give different weights and colour combinations, or mixed with another thread. Some threads are not colourfast, so take this into consideration if the embroidered item is to be washed. If in doubt, work a few stitches on a spare piece of fabric and wash it to check that the colour is fast.

Two of the most useful threads are stranded cotton, which can be divided into separate strands, and pearl cotton which is twisted and must be used as a single thread.

TRANSFERRING A DESIGN TO FABRIC

① Use dressmaker's carbon paper in a suitable colour for your fabric. It will work well on most fabrics and it is quick and easy to use.

② A transfer pencil will give a similar result to a commercial transfer. Take care to match the iron temperature to the composition of the fabric.

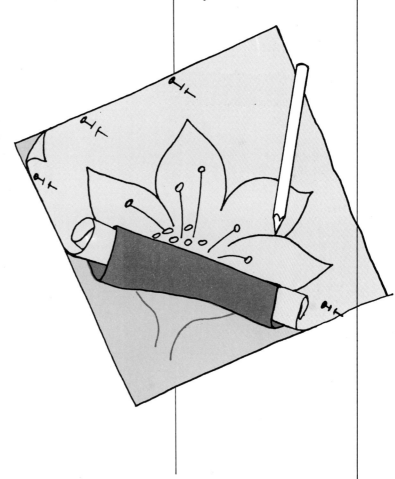

EMBROIDERY STITCHES

HERRINGBONE STITCH

Herringbone stitch is a line stitch that makes a pretty, crossed zigzag line and the stitches must be perfectly regular. It is worked from left to right and is very easy and quick to work. Guidelines may need to be marked on the fabric to keep the row straight. When the stitch is used as a filling, the rows can be placed so that the tips of the stitches on each row touch those on the row immediately preceding them. This will give a light trellis effect. For a heavier look, arrange the rows underneath each other so that the zigzags interlock. Herringbone stitch is also used as the foundation row for a number of more complicated stitches. Any type of thread can be used for this stitch, the choice depending on the size of stitch required and the weight of the ground fabric.

CHAIN STITCH

Chain stitch is one of the oldest embroidery stitches. Its use is widespread, and examples of the stitch can be found on many antique and contemporary textiles throughout the world.

Chain stitch forms a line stitch on plain- and even-weave fabrics. It can also be worked solidly to produce a dense filling, which lends itself well to shading. It is a simple stitch to work, but care should be taken to keep the stitches even and of the same size. Chain stitch makes a good outline stitch and is very useful for defining curves and intricate shapes when worked quite small. Any thread is suitable, but the size of the stitch will depend on the weight of the embroidery thread used. When used as a filling, chain stitch can either be worked in close rows to fill the shape, or the rows can be worked from the centre outwards in a spiral, using one or more colours or textures. Chain stitch can have a row of back stitch worked down the centre, in the same or a contrasting colour. Chain stitch can also be worked singly and it is then known as detached chain stitch or lazy daisy stitch.

CROSS STITCH

Cross stitch is probably the oldest and best known of all decorative embroidery stitches. It has many variations and has been known world-wide for centuries. Cross stitch is still used on traditional embroideries in many areas, including the Greek Islands, Scandinavia, Central and Eastern Europe and India.

It is extremely quick and easy to work and is used mainly on even-weave fabrics where the threads can be counted to keep the crosses even. The stitch can also be used on plain-weave fabrics, but guidelines will need to be marked on the fabric unless a commercially produced transfer is being used. Among its many uses, cross stitch is excellent for outlines, solid fillings, formalized motifs, borders and lettering. The top diagonal stitches must always fall in the same direction, unless a deliberate light-and-shade effect is required, in which case their direction can be varied to catch the light. Work a complete cross stitch before proceeding to the next stitch to form neat, slightly raised crosses.

STEM STITCH

Stem stitch is one of the most frequently used outline stitches. It is quite easy to work and follows curves and intricate linear details well. It can also be used for filling and shading areas.

The stitch is simply worked with a forwards and backwards motion along the line. The stitches should be evenly worked and equally sized. The working thread must always be kept at the right of the needle; if it is at the left, the effect is slightly different. A slightly wider stem stitch line can be made by inserting the needle into the fabric at a slight angle to the line instead of directly along it. Any type of embroidery thread can be used, providing that it is compatible with the size of the stitch and the weight of the ground fabric.

FEATHER STITCH

Feather stitch is a decorative line stitch used on plain- and even-weave fabrics. This stitch has been extensively used on traditional English smocks, both as a smocking stitch and as surface embroidery; it is also used as a decorative joining stitch on hand-sewn crazy patchwork.

It makes a pretty, feathery line, which is equally effective when worked in straight lines or following curves. Worked downwards, it is a quick stitch, easy to perfect. The thread is brought through at the top of the line to be covered and a slanting loop stitch is made alternately to the left and to the right of the line. Any type of embroidery thread can be used with feather stitch but the effect required and the weight of the ground fabric must be taken into account.

FANCY HERRINGBONE STITCH

Fancy herringbone stitch is a wide, ornamental line stitch used on plain- and even-weave fabrics. It makes a rich border, particularly if a metallic thread is used for the interlacing, and it can look stunning if worked in spaced multiple rows, using a carefully chosen colour scheme.

It is deceptively simple to work, in spite of its rather complex appearance. Each row is worked in three journeys. First, a foundation row of herringbone stitch is worked, using guidelines marked on the fabric. A row of upright cross stitches is then worked over the top and bottom crosses of the herringbone rows, taking care that the horizontal bar of the cross stitch is always worked over the vertical one. These two journeys can be worked in the same colour thread, or two contrasting threads. On the third journey, the horizontal bars are interlaced without the ground fabric being picked up. Use a blunt-ended tapestry needle for the interlacing to avoid splitting the stitches on the two preceding rows.

FLY STITCH

Fly stitch is an isolated stitch often worked in rows. Each stitch is worked very easily: a V-shaped loop is made and then tied down by a vertical straight stitch. The tying stitch can vary in length to produce different effects. The fly stitches can be arranged side by side to make a horizontal row, or worked underneath each other to make a vertical row. The stitches can touch one another or be spaced apart at a regular interval. Isolated fly stitches can be used to make a pretty powdering, either spaced evenly or scattered at random over a shape. Each stitch can be decorated by the addition of a Chinese knot in a contrasting thread. Any type of thread can be used for this stitch although the size of the stitch and the weight of the ground fabric must be taken into account.

TÊTE DE BOEUF FILLING STITCH

Tête de boeuf filling stitch is used on plain- and even-weave fabrics. It looks like a bull's head, complete with the horns. A fly stitch makes the horns, and a single chain stitch anchors the fly stitch and makes the head. It is usually worked in formal rows to make an attractive light filling but the stitch can also be worked in horizontal rows to form a border.

There appears to be some confusion about exactly which embroidery stitch is called tête de boeuf filling stitch. In some modern books tête de boeuf filling stitch appears under the name of detached wheat ear stitch even though it looks exactly like a bull's head. However, the stitch described above can be found in many Victorian needlework books, including Caulfield and Saward's 1887 edition of *The Dictionary of Needlework: An Encyclopedia of Artistic, Plain and Fancy Needlework,* where a wood engraving of it and the reference 'Tête de boeuf stitch' can be seen.

PEKINESE STITCH

Pekinese stitch is a composite line stitch used on plain- and even-weave fabrics. One of the principal stitches used on old Chinese embroideries, it was worked on a tiny scale, and was reputed to affect the eyesight of the worker, hence its alternative name, blind stitch. It was worked in silk and used to fill shapes solidly with carefully blended shades. Pekinese stitch makes an attractive braided line which follows any linear design well, and can be used as a filling stitch in the Chinese manner.

SATIN STITCH

Satin stitch is a line and filling stitch used on plain- and even-weave fabrics. It is one of the oldest embroidery stitches and, like cross stitch, examples of satin stitch can be found worked on traditional embroideries in practically every country, but notably in China and Japan.

Satin stitch consists of straight stitches worked side by side and, although it appears to be an easy stitch to work, some practice is required to work satin stitch evenly. It should be worked on fabric stretched in an embroidery hoop to prevent the material from puckering, and the stitches should lie evenly and closely together to cover the ground fabric completely. When used as a line stitch, it is worked between two lines with the stitches either slanting or at right angles to the lines to give a perfectly smooth surface. When worked as a filling, the stitches are taken right across the shape and can be worked vertically or diagonally, with changes of direction giving the effect of light and shade. This effect is enhanced by the use of a lustrous thread such as stranded cotton or silk but any embroidery thread can be used, the choice depending on the effect required and the weight of the ground fabric.

CHINESE KNOT

The Chinese knot is an isolated stitch which closely resembles the better known French knot, although the Chinese knot is flatter and more shapely. Chinese knots are characteristic of the rich silk embroideries of China, where they were worked very small and massed together to texture large areas. They were often worked in rows to create beautiful borders, with each row set close to the next one. Subtle colour variations in the silk thread resulted in a delicate shading. The alternative name blind knot reputedly derives from the fact that Chinese embroiderers stitched this knot on such a minute scale over large areas of fabric that eventually their eyesight was affected.

The Chinese knot is easy to work, especially if the fabric is stretched in an embroidery hoop. A simple, loose loop is made round the needle and tightened after the needle has entered the fabric but before it is pulled right through. Hold the loop down on the fabric with the left thumb, while pulling the needle through the fabric. This stitch works well with any type of embroidery thread; choose the thread according to the effect required. A stranded cotton or silk will give a flatter knot, while a rounded thread such as pearl cotton or tapestry wool will make a raised knot.

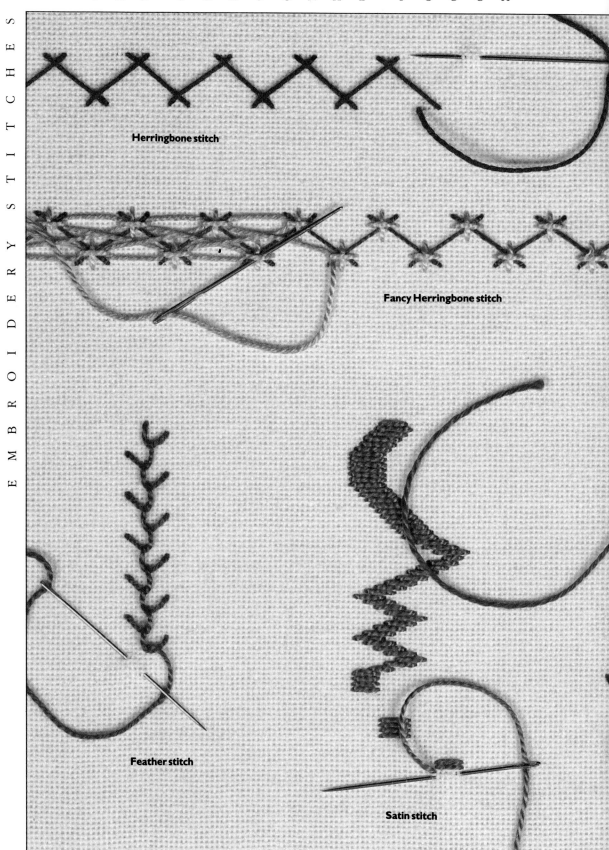

Herringbone stitch

Fancy Herringbone stitch

Feather stitch

Satin stitch

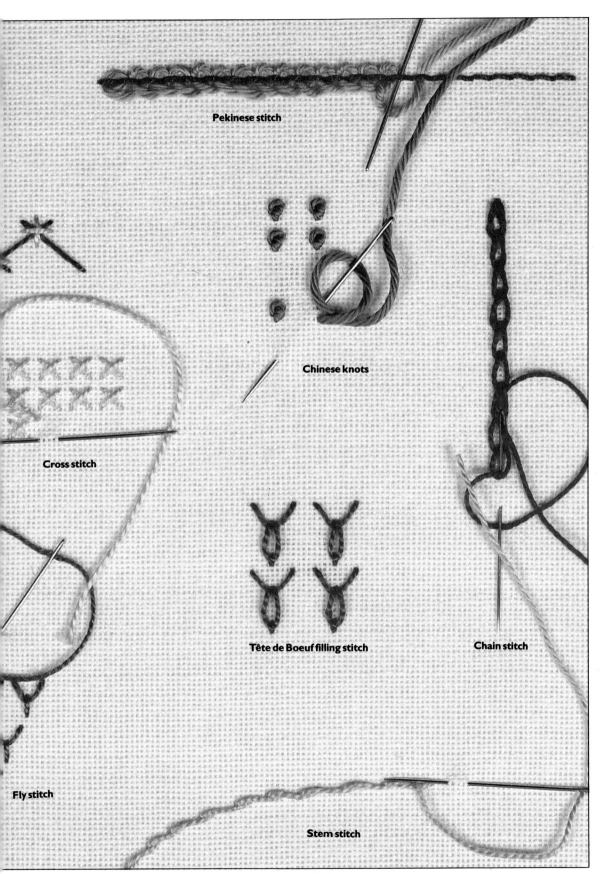

Pekinese stitch

Chinese knots

Cross stitch

Tête de Boeuf filling stitch

Chain stitch

Fly stitch

Stem stitch

MACHINE QUILTING

There are two distinct types of quilting that can be worked successfully by machine. In the first type, known as wadded or English quilting, two layers of fabric are separated by a layer of wadding and then all three layers are stitched together in a design. This type of quilting can add warmth to a garment or bed-cover as well as decoration. In the second type – raised or Italian quilting – only two layers of fabric are used, and the quilting is purely decorative. Two lines of parallel stitching make a narrow channel in the fabric and a fine cord is then inserted into the channel to make it stand out from the background fabric.

Choose simple, bold designs to quilt by machine and use closely woven, soft fabrics that are washable. Slippery and synthetic fabrics are tricky to handle and do not quilt well by machine. Polyester wadding is ideal to use for wadded quilting as it will wash well without losing any depth. Never press a quilted item as it will become flattened.

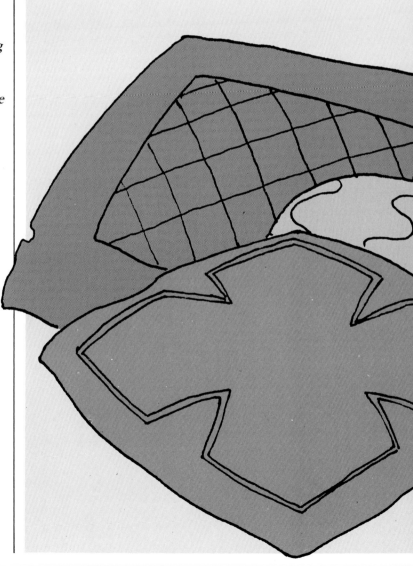

WADDED QUILTING

① Mark the design on to the right side of the top layer of fabric with a removable dressmaker's marker. Sandwich the wadding between the two fabric layers and tack them together. Work the tacking stitches horizontally and vertically at 10cm (4in) intervals across the layers, working from the centre outwards in each direction. Finish by working two diagonal lines from corner to corner.

② Loosen the pressure on the machine to allow the tacked layers to pass easily beneath the foot. Stitch carefully along the design lines using straight stitch; pay particular attention to curves and corners. Remove the tacking stitches when the quilting is completed.

RAISED QUILTING

① Mark the design on to the right side of the top layer of fabric with a removable dressmaker's marker. Tack the two layers of fabric together as for wadded quilting, with the wrong sides facing.
② Stitch along the design lines using a widely spaced twin needle and straight stitch. If your machine will not take a twin needle, work the two rows of stitching separately with an ordinary needle.
③ Remove the tacking stitches and thread pre-shrunk, fine piping cord through the channels using a blunt-ended tapestry needle. At each corner, pull needle through and reinsert, as shown.

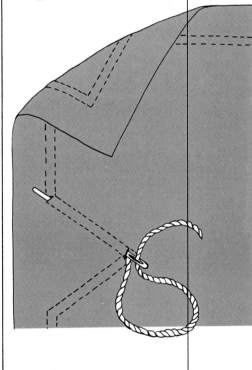

MACHINE APPLIQUÉ

Appliqué or applied work is a technique in which a motif cut from one piece of fabric is placed on to a fabric background and stitched in place around the edges. The stitching can be decorative and hand worked, or stitched by machine.

Machine-stitched appliqué is hard wearing and probably best for garments and home furnishings. Match the weight and fibre content of the applied fabrics to that of the background, especially if the item is to be washed. Choose plain or patterned fabrics and cut the motifs on the straight grain where possible to avoid stretching. Apply the motifs before making up, unless you are adding them to an existing item.

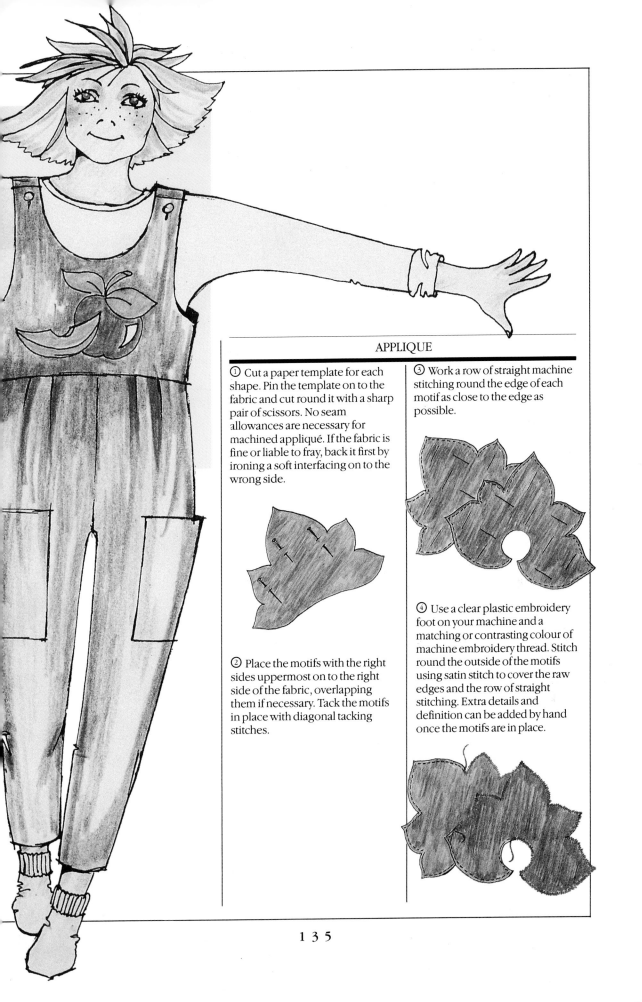

APPLIQUE

① Cut a paper template for each shape. Pin the template on to the fabric and cut round it with a sharp pair of scissors. No seam allowances are necessary for machined appliqué. If the fabric is fine or liable to fray, back it first by ironing a soft interfacing on to the wrong side.

② Place the motifs with the right sides uppermost on to the right side of the fabric, overlapping them if necessary. Tack the motifs in place with diagonal tacking stitches.

③ Work a row of straight machine stitching round the edge of each motif as close to the edge as possible.

④ Use a clear plastic embroidery foot on your machine and a matching or contrasting colour of machine embroidery thread. Stitch round the outside of the motifs using satin stitch to cover the raw edges and the row of straight stitching. Extra details and definition can be added by hand once the motifs are in place.

MACHINE PATCHWORK

Patchwork is the art of stitching together small pieces of fabric to make a larger piece. One of the main attractions of patchwork is that you can use up scraps of fabric which are too small for anything else. Traditionally, patchwork was sewn by hand using paper templates, but good results can be achieved using a machine. The process is much faster and the results are much more durable than the hand-sewn type. You can use the finished patchwork just like a piece of ordinary fabric, although it will need to be lined to hide the raw edges. Patchwork looks good if it is wadded and quilted along the outlines of the patches.

Closely woven cottons and cotton/polyester blends are the best fabrics to use as they do not slip and are easy to stitch. With care, you can combine different types of fabric but try to keep the weights fairly similar to avoid distortion and puckering. Keep the size of the patches reasonably large as patches with sides less than 4cm (1½in) long are tricky to sew by machine. The most successful shapes for machined patchwork are squares, rectangles and triangles. These shapes can be combined to make a variety of patterns, as shown.

The traditional patterns have colourful names such as cotton reel, Jacob's ladder, Flying Dutchman and Sherman's march. Each of the blocks shown can be repeated to make a larger piece of patchwork, and they should be divided into sections for ease of assembly. Work the sections separately and then join them together to create the finished block.

SQUARES

Hit and miss
Castellated pattern
Framed squares

SQUARES	RECTANGLES	
Checkerboard Going down stairs Strip pattern	Checks Brick wall Zigzag bricks	Turned rectangles Up and down Roman squares

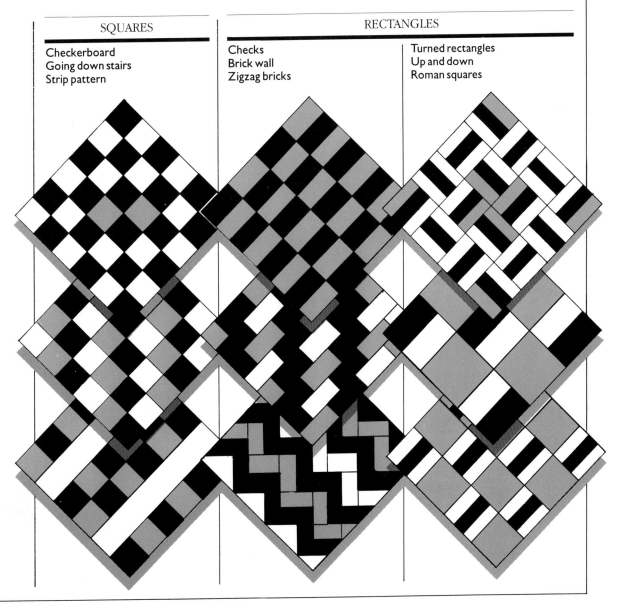

TRIANGLES

TRIANGLES AND SQUARES

High noon
Railroad crossing
Cotton reel
Birds in air

Jacob's ladder
Water wheel
Winged square
Ohio star

Shark's tooth square
Double T
Handy Andy
Boxed square

Rising star
Eight hand round
Lemoyne star
54-40

Greek cross block
Flying Dutchman
Tall pine tree
Weather vane

Red cross
Goose in the pond
Sherman's march
Rolling stone

CUTTING THE PATCHES

① You will need to cut two accurate templates from stiff card for every shape you are using. One template should be the size of the finished patch and the other should be 1cm (³⁄₈in) larger all round. Cut the two sizes of template from different colours of card to avoid getting them mixed up when cutting the fabric.

② If you wish to centralize a fabric motif, cut a template with a cut-out window the finished size of the patch. Move it round on the fabric until it is in the right position and mark the fabric lightly round the window using a soft pencil.

③ Work out how many patches of each shape and colour you need for the finished piece. Using the large templates and working on the wrong side of the fabric, draw round the shapes on the appropriate fabric with a soft pencil to mark the cutting line. Cut out the shapes and keep each colour and shape of patch in separate piles.

④ Centre the smaller template on the wrong side of the fabric patch and draw round it with a pencil to mark the stitching lines. Keep the pencil sharp and follow the template shape carefully.

JOINING THE PATCHES

① Pin and tack the patches together, following the sequence described below. Stitch along the pencil line and fasten off the threads at each end of the seam. Press each seam to one side before adding the next patch, preferably pressing the seam away from any lightly coloured patches. Remove the tacking stitches.

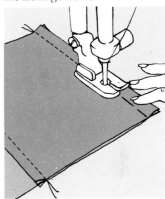

② Begin joining the patches together in pairs, and then add further patches until you have completed one section of the block. Join the sections together to make up the finished block. Join the blocks into strips, and join the strips together to make the finished piece of patchwork.

MACHINE CRAZY PATCHWORK

Crazy patchwork is the original form of patchwork and it was
probably invented as an economy measure to make something useful
from worn out garments. It is assembled rather like a jigsaw from
randomly shaped patches which are pinned, tacked and then stitched
on to a firm cotton backing fabric.

① Begin placing the patches at one corner of the backing fabric, starting with a right-angled patch. Gradually build up the design by placing the patches in turn on the backing so that they overlap the edges of the previous patches.

② The design can be worked in sections, pinning and tacking one area before moving on to the next, or all the patches can be laid out before they are pinned.

③ When all the patches are tacked in place, work machine satin stitch over the raw edges. Use a clear plastic embroidery foot on the machine and take care to follow the outlines accurately.

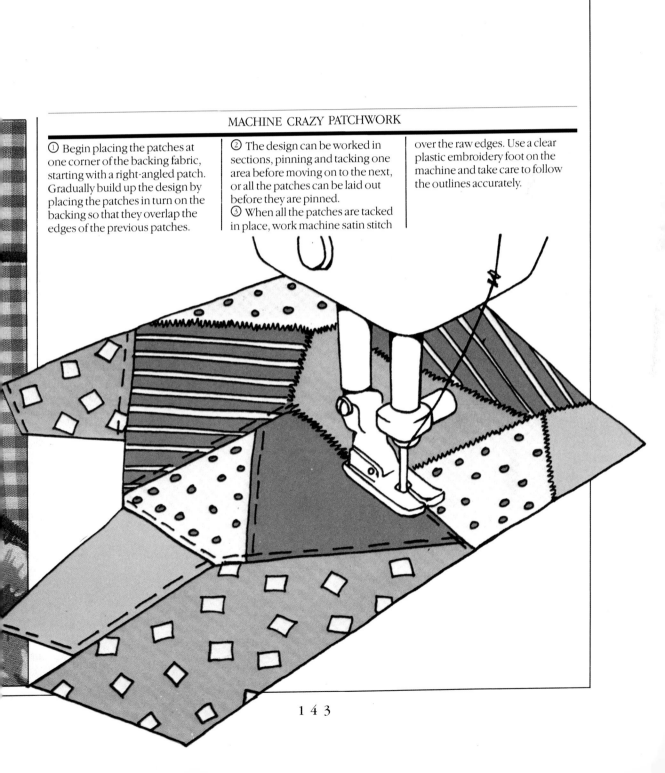

Many items of home furnishings are quite easy to make once you have mastered some of the basic sewing techniques described in Chapter 3. Bedlinen, duvets, tablecloths, curtains and cushions are less expensive to make than to buy, and you will have a much greater choice of fabrics and colours. This is especially important when you want to coordinate the colour scheme for a particular room.

T A B L E   L I N E N

STRAIGHT-SIDED TABLECLOTHS

These are the most common and useful types of tablecloth and they can be either square or rectangular. They can be simply finished and functional or be decorated with embroidery, appliqué, lace or braid. Patchwork tablecloths also look attractive.

① Measure the table top and decide how far you want the cloth to hang down over the sides. Add a 3cm (1¼in) hem allowance all round. If the fabric must be joined, avoid an unsightly seam down the

centre of the cloth. Cut out the centre panel first, then cut another piece the same length and cut it in half lengthways. Pin, tack and stitch each half width to the sides of the centre panel using a flat, self-neatening seam. Match any patterns on the fabric carefully.

② Press 1.5cm (⅝in) of the hem allowance to the wrong side along each side of the cloth. Fold over and press the second 1.5cm (⅝in) of the allowance. Open out the last hem fold and mitre the corners.
③ Pin, tack and stitch the hem by hand or machine. Alternatively, trim down the hem allowance to 5mm (¼in) and bind the raw edge of the cloth with a contrasting colour bias binding.

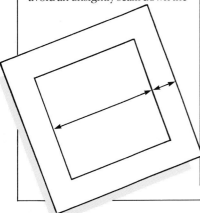

CIRCULAR TABLECLOTHS

Round tables look particularly attractive when dressed with a circular tablecloth. The cloth can just overlap the table top or it can reach the floor to give a more formal effect. Although it looks best if the cloth is cut from one width of fabric, it may need to be joined for a large table. Do this in the same way as for a straight-sided cloth.
① Measure the diameter of the table top first, and then the depth of the overhang. Double this measurement and add it to the diameter. Add 1.5cm (⅝in) all round for the hem allowance.
② Fold the fabric into quarters and draw a quarter circle the required size on to the fabric using a pencil and a piece of string, as shown. Alternatively, draw the quarter circle on to a piece of sturdy brown paper, cut it out and use this as a pattern for cutting the fabric. Cut out the fabric.

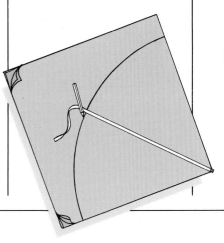

NAPKINS

The usual size of a napkin is between 45cm (18in) and 50cm (20in) square, but they can be made in any shape or size, depending on your preference.
① Cut out the napkins. On each napkin, turn a double 5mm (¼in) hem on all the edges, mitring the corners.
② Pin, tack and stitch round the hem. Alternatively, bind the edge with bias binding as for a tablecloth.

TABLE MATS

Table mats are usually rectangular, measuring 20cm (8in) by 30cm (12in). They can also be round and measure between 20cm (8in) and 25cm (10in) across. Table mats should be thick enough to afford some protection to the surface of the table, so a quilted fabric is ideal. Buy ready quilted fabric, or sandwich a thin layer of wadding between the top and bottom layers of fabric before finishing the raw edges. You could also quilt your own fabric by hand or machine or use a piece of patchwork for the front.
① Cut out two pieces of fabric and one of thin wadding to the required size, curving the corners slightly if the mat is rectangular.
② Place the fabric pieces together with the wrong sides facing, sandwiching the wadding in between. Pin the layers together and tack around the edge.
③ Bind the raw edges with bias binding, following the instructions for binding a continuous edge.

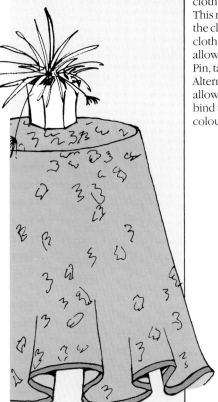

③ Stitch round the outside of the cloth 1.5cm (⅝in) from the edge. This marks the finished edge of the cloth. On the wrong side of the cloth, press under the hem allowance along the stitched line. Pin, tack and stitch the hem. Alternatively, trim down the hem allowance to 5mm (¼in) and bind the edge with a contrasting colour bias binding.

PILLOWCASES

The standard pillow size is 75cm (29½in) long by 50cm (20in) wide. Use a single piece of extra wide sheeting for each plain pillowcase.

① Double the length measurement and add 21cm (8in) for the flap and the hem allowances. Add 3cm (1¼in) seam allowance to the width. Cut out the fabric.

② Along one short edge, turn a double 5mm (¼in) hem to the wrong side. Pin, tack and stitch in place. On the opposite short edge, turn 5cm (2in) to the wrong side and turn under the raw edge for 1cm (⅜in). Pin, tack and stitch in place, close to the inner fold.

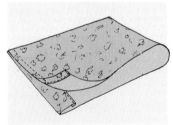

③ Lay the fabric out flat with the right side down. Fold in the edge with the narrow hem to make a 15cm (5½in) deep flap. Press and pin in place. Fold the fabric in half widthways with the wrong sides together, so that the other short edge with the wide hem is level with the flap fold. Pin, tack and stitch the side edges, taking a 5mm (¼in) seam allowance.

④ Turn the pillowcases so that the right sides are facing, as shown. Pin, tack and stitch down the sides again, 1cm (⅜in) from the seamed edge. Turn the pillowcase right side out.

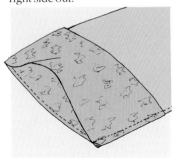

FRILLED PILLOWCASES

Frilled pillowcases are very decorative and the frills can be made from matching or contrasting fabric. Unlike a plain pillowcase, this type has separate pieces of fabric for the front, back and flap.

① Measure the pillow top both ways. Cut one back piece to this size, adding 6.5cm (2⅝in) to the length and 3cm (1¼in) to the width for the hem and seam allowances. Cut one front piece adding 3cm (1¼in) seam allowance all round. Cut one flap the same width as the front and back including the seam allowance and 17.5cm (7in) deep. Cut long strips of fabric for the frill to make a length twice that of the complete outer edge of the pillow. The depth of this strip should be twice the width of the finished frill (usually between 2cm (¾in) and 8cm (3in), plus 3cm (1¼in) for seam allowances.)

② Along one short edge of the back piece, turn under 5cm (2in) to the wrong side and then turn under 1cm (⅜in) along the raw edge. Pin, tack and stitch in place. Along one long edge of the flap, turn under a double 5mm (¼in) hem. Pin, tack and stitch in place. Pin, tack and stitch the frill pieces with the right sides facing into a circle, using flat seams.

③ Fold the frill in half lengthways with the wrong sides facing and pin. Divide the frill into four equal sections and mark with a tailor's tack. Gather each frill section in

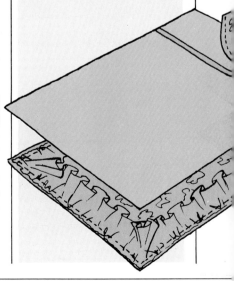

turn. Divide the complete edge of the front piece into four equal sections and mark. Position the frill on the right side of the front

with the frill facing inwards to the centre. Pull up the gathering stitches of each section in turn to match the sections on the pillowcase front. Match the marks on the front to those on the frill and then pin, tack and stitch the frill in place.

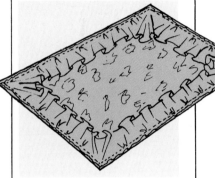

④ Assemble the pillowcase by placing the back on top of the frilled front with the right sides facing. Align the hemmed edge of the back with the seamline on the front. Place the flap right side down over the back, as shown, matching the long raw edge with the raw edge of the front. Pin, tack and stitch in place, following the previous line of stitching; take care not to catch the hemmed edge of the back in the stitching. Trim and neaten the raw edges, remove the tacking stitches, and turn right side out with the flap on the inside.

S
H
E
E
T
S

Wide width sheeting is now readily available in a variety of colours and patterns, so it is quite easy to make your own sheets, pillowcases and duvet covers to match the bedroom décor. Sheeting is made from either pure cotton or easy-care cotton/polyester blends. Bedspreads need not be laundered as frequently as sheets and duvet covers, so washability is not so important. Making a duvet is much cheaper than buying one and they can be filled with a natural or synthetic material.

FLAT SHEETS

Flat sheets are the simplest type of sheet to make.

① Measure the mattress across the top in both directions, adding twice the depth of the mattress and a 25cm (10in) tucking-in allowance to both these measurements. Add 21cm (8in) to the length and 4cm (1½in) to the width for the hem allowances, and cut out the fabric.

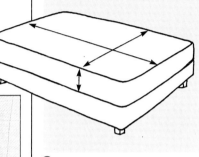

② Turn under a double 1cm (⅜in) hem to the wrong side along each side edge. Pin, tack and stitch in place. At the base end, turn a double 2.5cm (1in) hem to the wrong side, and pin, tack and stitch in place.

③ Turn a double 8cm (3in) hem to the wrong side along the top edge, and pin and tack in place. Using a cording foot, zigzag stitch over a length of fine cord approximately 1cm (⅜in) from the inner fold of the hem. Fasten each end of the cord securely. Alternatively, work two rows of straight stitching 3mm (⅛in) apart to form a channel. Thread the cord through the channel with a fine tapestry needle.

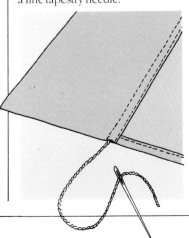

FITTED SHEETS

Fitted sheets have elasticated corners and they are often preferred to flat sheets because they do not come untucked. They need to be measured accurately to give a good fit.

① Measure the mattress top both ways and to both of these measurements add twice the mattress depth plus twice the tucking-in allowance of 18cm (7in). Cut out the fabric.

② Make each corner seam first. Measure the mattress depth plus 18cm (7in) along each side from the corner and mark. Measure in at right angles from the two marks as shown, and mark again. Fold the marked corner with the wrong sides facing; pin and tack. Cut off the corner of the fabric as shown leaving a 1.5cm (⅝in) seam allowance. Make a French seam along this edge to form the corner seam.

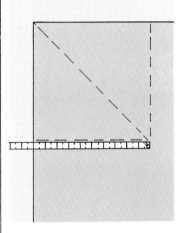

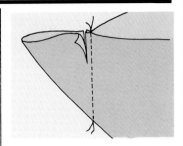

③ Turn under a double 1.5cm (⅝in) casing around the edge of the sheet and pin in place. Measure along the casing for 34cm (13½in) on either side of each corner seam and mark. Tack and stitch round the casing, leaving a 1.5cm (⅝in) opening at each mark.

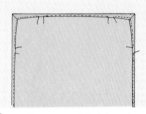

④ Cut four 23cm (9in) lengths of narrow elastic. Pin the end of one length of elastic at one opening inside the casing. Thread the opposite end of the elastic round the corner inside the casing and pin at the other opening.

⑤ Pin and stitch across the casing and ends of elastic just before the openings; use two rows of stitching to hold the elastic firmly in position. Stitch across the openings to close neatly. Repeat at each corner.

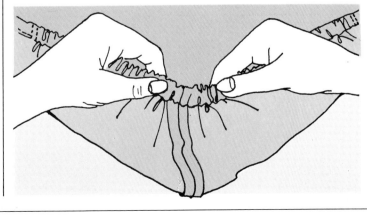

Duvets are warm, light and comfortable to sleep under, but they are quite expensive to buy. They are fairly easy to make at home and considerably cheaper. A duvet is a fabric bag divided into walled channels and filled with a natural or synthetic filling. If using a feather filling, use downproof cambric with the shiny side inside for the bag; if using a synthetic filling, use a plain cotton sheeting. 5cm (2in) wide white cotton tape is used for the walls of the channels.

Traditionally, duvets are filled with sterilized duck or goose down, either on its own or mixed with feathers for economy. Synthetic fillings have the advantage of being washable, so they are ideal to use for children's quilts, as well as for people who are allergic to feathers.

The fabric bag is made in exactly the same way for both natural and synthetic fillings, but the method of filling is slightly different. A double duvet measures 200cm (80in) by 200cm (80in), and a single duvet is 140cm (55in) by 200cm (80in). If the fabric has to be joined, use a flat, self-neatening seam.

① Cut out two pieces of fabric to the size of the duvet, adding a 2cm (³⁄₄in) seam allowance all round. On the wrong side of each piece of fabric, mark a 2cm (³⁄₄in) margin all round.
② Mark the position of the channels on each piece of fabric between these margins. Rule lines with tailor's chalk to divide the width into equal sections. On a single duvet make five 28cm (11in) sections, and on a double duvet make eight 25cm (10in) sections. Cut a 204cm (81½in) length of cotton tape for each marked line on one piece of fabric.
③ Working on one piece of fabric, place the first length of tape over the first marked line, overlapping it by 5mm (¼in). Tack and stitch the tape to the fabric 5mm (¼in) from the edge of the tape. Repeat this with the remaining lengths of tape. Place the two pieces of fabric together with the right sides facing, matching the side edges.

Pin, tack and stitch along one margin line parallel to the tapes to make the first side seam.

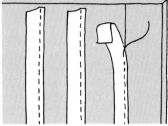

④ Working away from the stitched side seam, join the free edge of the first piece of tape to the second piece of fabric, again overlapping the marked line by 5mm (¼in). Repeat this on each free edge of tape, as shown.

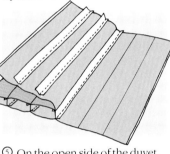

⑤ On the open side of the duvet, fold both pieces of fabric together into a double 1cm (³⁄₈in) hem. Pin, tack and stitch along the hem twice, the first time close to the fold and the second about 5mm (¼in) away from the fold. Hem the base edge of the duvet in the same way. Along the stitched side seam, work two rows of topstitching to match the stitching on the hemmed side edge.

Allow the following amount of filling per channel:
Pure down – 150g (5oz)
Down and feather – 175g (6oz)
Feather and down – 200g (7oz)
Synthetic filling – 200g (7oz)
① Peg the top edge of the duvet to a clothes line, making sure that the channels are open. If you are using a feather filling, put a handful of filling into each channel in turn, closing the channel with a peg after each handful. Repeat this until all the filling has been used.
② For a synthetic filling, first divide it into equal portions for each channel. Fill each channel in turn, pinning them closed after they are filled.
③ In both cases, fold the open edges together to make a double 1cm (³⁄₈in) hem. Tack and stitch twice to match the other edges.

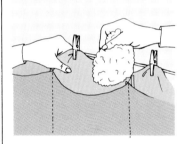

DUVET COVERS

DUVET COVERS

A duvet cover is essential to keep the duvet clean in use. Use a wide width cotton or cotton/polyester sheeting for the cover. You will also need a length of press stud tape to close the cover. Alternatively, you could use touch and close fastening discs, press studs or ribbon ties. Covers for duvets are made the same size as the duvet itself: single size – 200cm (80in) by 140cm (55in), double size – 200cm (80in) square.

① Cut out two pieces of fabric to the required size, adding a seam allowance of 9cm (3⅝in) to the length and 3cm (1¼in) to the width. Fold a double 2.5cm (1in) hem along the base edge of both pieces. Pin, tack and stitch in place.

② Place the two pieces of fabric together with the right sides facing, matching the hemmed edges. Pin, tack and stitch them together along the inner edge of hem for 30cm (12in) in from the side edges, to make a central opening.

③ Place a length of press stud tape along one half of the hem opening. Pin, tack and stitch in place. Repeat this for the other side of the opening, making sure that the press studs align.

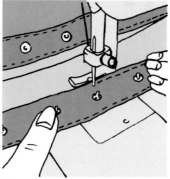

④ Fold the cover with the right sides facing. Pin, tack and stitch twice vertically across the hem at each side of the opening to enclose the raw edges of the tape. Fold the cover with the wrong sides facing and make a French seam round the other three sides. Turn the cover to the right side.

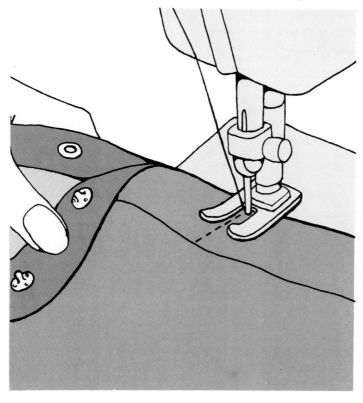

There are three main types of bed coverings: throwover bedspreads, fitted bedspreads with a gathered frill and tailored bedspreads. A throwover bedspread is simply a flat piece of fabric that is draped over the bed, and this is the easiest type to make. The other two are more formal.

They all have a full fabric width on the top, to which side panels will need to be attached to give the correct width for a double bed. Cut out two fabric widths to the required length, allowing extra on the length for matching the pattern if necessary. Cut the second piece in half lengthways and join the half widths to the sides of the centre width with a flat seam. Neaten the raw edges of the seams.

Any type of fabric can be used for a bedspread, but a firm fabric will give a better result than a fine, delicate one and it will not need to be lined, except for a gathered fitted bedspread. You should always make up the bed fully before measuring it to estimate the fabric requirements.

THROWOVER BEDSPREAD

This simple bedspread should be large enough to cover the bed and reach to the floor. The corners can be rounded to give it a neater appearance and the seam along the bed top can be piped in a matching or contrasting fabric.
① Measure the made-up bed widthways to the floor on either side. Measure lengthways from the bed head to the floor. Add a 5cm (2in) hem allowance all round.
② Cut out the fabric, and join it if necessary. Turn 5cm (2in) to the wrong side and turn under the raw edge for 1cm (⅜in). Press the hem and mitre the corners. Pin, tack and hem by hand. Remove the tacking and press the hem.

GATHERED FITTED BEDSPREAD

This type of bedspread is very pretty, but it needs much more fabric than a throwover spread and it is quite complicated to make.
① Measure the top of the bed both ways and add 20cm (7¾in) to the length for the tuck-in and 3cm (1¼in) seam allowances to the width. To calculate the length of the frill, add twice the bed-top length to the bed-top width and then double this measurement to allow for the gathering. For the depth of the frill, measure from the bed top to within 1cm (⅜in) of the floor and add 3cm (1¼in) for the seam allowances. The length of fabric for the frill will need to be joined, so allow extra fabric for the seams and matching the pattern if necessary.

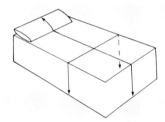

② Cut out the fabric and then cut out a second set of pieces from lining fabric. For the lining, use a soft cotton fabric that tones with the main fabric.
③ Round off the fabric and lining for the bed top at the base corners. To do this, draw round a plate and then cut along the marked line. Join the fabric frill pieces together with flat seams and repeat this for the frill lining. Press the seams well.
④ Place the fabric and lining frill pieces together with the right

sides facing. Pin, tack and stitch them together along the side and base edges. Turn the frill to the right side and press. Pin and tack the top raw edges together.
⑤ Divide the length of the frill into six equal sections and mark them with tailor's tacks. Divide the side and base edges of the bedspread top into six equal sections and mark in the same way. Work two rows of gathering stitches between the marks on the frill in turn, and pull up each section of gathering to fit the marked sections on the top.
⑥ Place the frill on the bedspread top with the right sides facing with the sides of the frill 1.5cm (⅝in) from the straight edge of the bed top. Pin, tack and stitch the frill in place.
⑦ Pin, tack and stitch the top straight edges of the lining and fabric bedspread top together, with the right sides facing. Press the seam and turn the lining down over the wrong side of the top. Turn under the side and base edges of the lining and pin to the wrong side of the frill, covering the previous line of stitching and the raw edges. Tack the lining in position and slip stitch it to the lining of the frill.

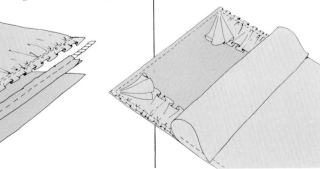

TAILORED BEDSPREAD

This type of fitted bedspread is quite plain in construction and looks best with the pillows placed on top rather than underneath. It has plain sides, and the seam around the top can be piped to give a crisper finish.
① Cut out one piece of fabric for the bedspread top to the measurement of the bed top, adding a 4.5cm (1⅞in) to the length and 3cm (1¼in) to the width for seam allowances. For a double bed, you will need to join the two lengths of fabric to get the correct width. For the depth of sides, measure the distance from the bed top to within 1cm (⅜in) of the floor and add a 6.5cm (2⅝in) hem and seam allowance. Measure the side edges of the bedspread top and the base edge, and add 3cm (1¼in) to each measurement. Cut out two pieces of fabric for the sides and one for the base.
② Join the side and base pieces to make a long strip, using flat seams and taking a 1.5cm (⅝in) allowance. Press the seams. Turn a double 2.5cm (1in) hem along the lower long edge and pin, tack and stitch it in place. Press the hem.

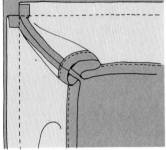

③ With the right sides facing, pin the strip to the top. Match the seams to the corners and, before stitching the corners, undo 1.5cm (⅝in) of the seams on the strip to allow the fabric to lay flat. Stitch taking 1.5cm (⅝in) seams, and pivot the fabric when stitching the corners. Press the seams towards the top and neaten the raw edges.
④ Turn a double 1.5cm (⅝in) hem along the top edge of the bedspread and pin, tack and stitch it in place.

Cushion pads can be bought ready made, but the shapes and sizes available are rather limited. They are quick to make and you can make virtually any shape, including rectangles, circles, triangles, stars and shell shapes. Fill them with either a feather and down mixture or a loose polyester fibre filling which is less expensive. Foam chips are also available but they tend to be rather hard and lumpy. An old feather pillow or eiderdown makes a good source of cushion filling. If you are using a feather filling, make the cover of the pad from featherproof cambric with the shiny side inside. For other fillings, a strong cotton calico is adequate.

CUSHION PADS

As a guide, for a 45cm (18in) square cushion you will need approximately 1kg (2.2lb) of feather and down mixture or 450g (1lb) of polyester fibre filling.

① Cut out two pieces of fabric to the required shape and size, adding 3cm (1¼in) all round for the seam allowance. Place the pieces with the right sides together and pin, tack and stitch round the edge, leaving an opening of at least 20cm (7¾in) centrally in one side.

② Stitch round a second time to strengthen the seam. Trim the seam allowance down to 1.5cm (⅝in) and turn the cover to the right side. Fill the cover firmly. Take care to stuff the corners of triangular and star-shaped cushions firmly. Turn in the raw edges of the opening in line with the seam and slip stitch to close. Use small stitches and a strong thread to prevent the pad from splitting.

RECTANGULAR CUSHION COVERS

Basic rectangular cushion covers are easy to make and they can quickly provide a splash of colour in a room. For decoration, add piping or a frill in a contrasting colour or type of fabric.

① Measure the cushion pad each way. Cut out two pieces of fabric to the required size and add a 1.5cm (⅝in) seam allowance all round. Place the two pieces of fabric together with the right sides facing, and pin, tack and stitch together all round, leaving an opening centrally in one side.

② Trim down the seam allowance to 1cm (⅜in) and cut across the corners close to the stitching. Neaten the raw edges. Turn the cover to the right side.

③ Insert the cushion pad. Turn in the raw edges of the opening in line with the seam and slip stitch to close. If you want to remove the cushion cover for laundering without having to unpick the stitches each time, there are various alternative ways of closing the opening.

OPENINGS

① Make an opening across the centre of the cushion back by making a flat seam and inserting a centred standard zip into it. This

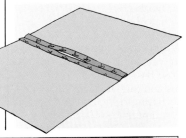

works especially well on a piped cushion. You will need to add an extra 3cm (1¼in) to the seam allowance on the back when cutting out the fabric to allow for the centre zipped seam. Omit the side opening when making up the cover.

② Follow the instructions given for making a plain pillowcase, but make the flap much deeper.

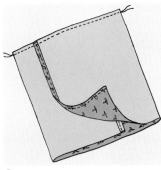

③ Use press stud tape or a length of touch and close fastening to fasten a side opening. Make the opening on the cushion cover in the same way as for a duvet cover.

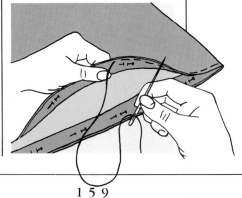

SHAPED CUSHION COVERS

Shaped cushion covers are made in the same way as rectangular ones. The opening can be along one edge or on the centre of the back, depending on your preference.

Cut out two pieces of fabric to the identical size and shape of the cushion pad plus 1.5cm (⅝in) seam allowances all round. Make as for a rectangular cover.

CURTAINS

Making your own curtains is much more economical than buying ready made ones and the choice of curtain fabrics is extensive, varying from heavy and luxurious velvet to light and frothy sheers. New curtains can transform a room quickly and relatively cheaply, to become an interesting feature of the décor instead of a mere window covering.

Curtains can be lined or unlined, but a lining will make them more draughtproof and help to prevent them from fading. Some cotton curtain fabrics are not pre-shrunk, so if you intend to wash them rather than have them dry cleaned, make a deeper hem that can be unpicked if the fabric does shrink. Check for washability and possible shrinkage when you buy the fabric, as many manufacturers now state the shrinkage allowance on the fabric composition label.

CURTAIN TRACKS

There is a wide variety of curtain tracks available in many styles and finishes. They are made from either metal or plastic and come in different colours to match both the style of the room and the design of the curtains. Each length of track will include the fittings to fix the track to the wall, end stops, runners and fixing instructions. On some types of track the hooks will also be included, otherwise these must be purchased separately. Extras for curtain tracks include pull cords for the curtains, which are useful if the track is to be fixed high up, overlap arms to provide a good central closure and brackets to hold the track further away from the wall.

CURTAIN POLES

As with tracks, curtain poles come in a range of styles and materials. Brass poles are attractive although rather expensive. Natural wooden poles are cheaper and more versatile as they can be sealed, stained or painted to match the décor. The poles come in a range of lengths and diameters and they are usually sold complete with fixing brackets, rings and fixing instructions. The rings have screw eyes attached for holding the curtain hooks. Always use the highest pocket in the heading tape for the hooks so that the curtains hang below the pole rather than in front.

Some shops will cut the fabric you buy into matched lengths ready for sewing. This is very useful if you are rather nervous about the amount of extra fabric to allow for matching patterns correctly. Check your measurements carefully before purchasing curtain fabric.

Curtains can be made in various lengths depending on the effect required. Sill length curtains are popular for kitchens and bedrooms, while floor length curtains are often used in living areas. Alternatively, the curtains can hang from a brass or wooden pole halfway up the window. These are known as café curtains.

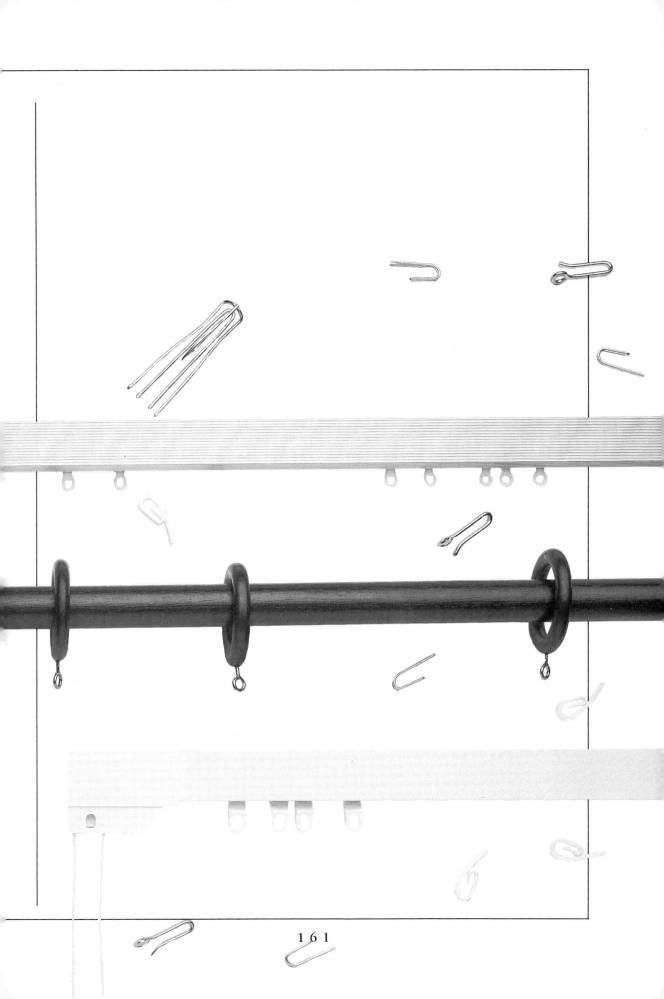

Heading tapes are strips of strong fabric which are stitched across the top of the curtain. They gather the fabric and provide pockets to hold the hooks which attach the curtains to the track or pole. The type of heading used will affect the look of the curtains, so it is important to choose the right sort of tape. Different headings require varying amounts of fabric.

STANDARD TAPE

Standard tape is the simplest and most economical heading to use. It is fairly narrow and gathers the fabric randomly for an informal look. This type of heading needs about one and a half times the track length of fabric. Standard heading is ideal for use on unlined curtains, as it comes in different colours and can be used on all types of fabric. There is a special lightweight standard tape for use with nets and sheer fabric.

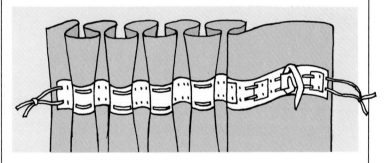

PENCIL PLEAT TAPE

This type of tape is probably the most popular as it gathers the fabric into regular tight pleats. It can be used on all weights of fabric and requires between two and a quarter and two and a half times the track length of fabric. It is available in various widths and has two or three lines of pockets so that the hooks can be placed in different positions to suit the type of track.

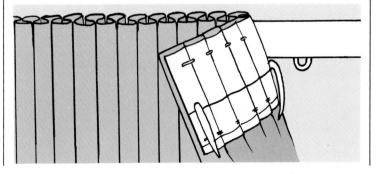

CARTRIDGE PLEAT TAPE

This type of tape is particularly suitable for use with heavy fabrics such as velvet and brocade. It gathers the fabric into evenly spaced rounded pleats and requires two and a half times the track length of fabric.

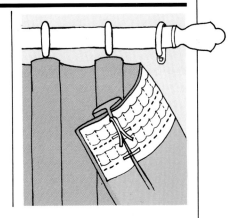

TRIPLE PLEAT TAPE

Triple pleat tape gathers the fabric into groups of three pleats at intervals along the curtain to give a formal look. It needs twice the track length of fabric.

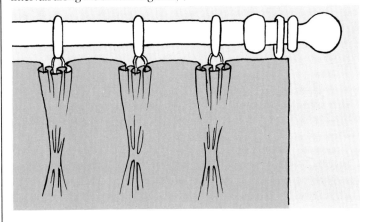

LINING TAPE

Lining tape is designed specially to attach a detachable lining to a curtain. The lining is sandwiched between the two layers of the tape and the lining tape is then hooked on to the curtain tape. It requires about one and a half times the track length of lining.

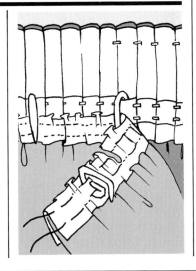

MEASURING UP AND CUTTING FABRIC

MEASURING WINDOWS

① Fix the track or pole above the window before you begin to measure.

② Decide which heading tape you will be using as this will determine how many track lengths of fabric you need. Divide the total width needed by the fabric width (usually 120cm (47/48in) if you are using furnishing fabric) to find out how many widths will cover the track.

③ To find the length of each fabric drop, measure from the track to where you want the curtain to end. If the curtains are to be floor length, deduct 1.5cm (⅝in) to allow the curtain to clear the floor. Add the allowance for the top (depending on the heading tape you are using) and at least 15cm (5½in) for the hem. If the fabric is patterned you will also need to add the length of one pattern repeat for each drop after the first one. This will allow you to match the patterns correctly.

④ Multiply the length of the drop by the number of fabric widths to find the total amount of fabric required.

⑤ You will also need to buy enough heading tape for the width of the curtain plus extra for turnings. If you are using cartridge or triple pleated tape, you will need to buy extra for positioning it so that the pleats will match across the curtains.

PLAIN FABRICS

① Straighten one cut edge of the fabric along the grain. Measure the first length from the straight cut edge and mark across the fabric using a metre stick and tailor's chalk. Cut across the marked line and repeat for each length.

② Cut any half widths of fabric by folding the fabric in half lengthways with the selvedges together. Carefully cut along the fold.

PATTERNED FABRICS

① Always place complete motifs along the base edge of the curtain, as any half motifs at the top will be hidden by the gathering. Mark the base of the pattern repeat and measure the hem allowance below this mark. Cut along this line.

② Place the cut length against the uncut fabric and match up the pattern across both widths. Mark and cut off the second length to match the first one. Repeat this for each fabric length. Cut any half lengths as for plain fabric. Mark the top of each length to make sure that they are all the same way up before you begin making up.

DETACHABLE LININGS

Detachable linings are made with a pocketed tape that shares the same hooks as the curtains. If your track has combined hooks and gliders, use standard hooks on the lining tape and slot them through the eyelets on the gliders.

① Cut out and make up the linings in the same way as for unlined curtains, apart from the top edge.
② Measure the length of the lining so that it will be 2.5cm (1in) shorter than the curtain. Mark this length at intervals across the width using a metre ruler and tailor's chalk. Cut across the marked line.
③ Slip the cut edge of the lining in between the two parts of the tape. Pin, tack and stitch along the tape.

Lined curtains look very professional and they will hang rather better than a curtain with a detachable lining. Circular curtain weights can be added to heavy fabrics at the corners of the curtain and at the base of each seam.

① Cut out the fabric as for unlined curtains, allowing 20cm (7¾in) for the base hem and heading, and 6.5cm (2½in) for each side hem. Cut out the lining in the same way, but cut it 15cm (5½in) shorter and 13cm (5in) narrower than the curtain fabric.

② If necessary, join the fabric widths in the same way as for unlined curtains and then repeat this for the lining. On the curtain fabric, turn in 6.5cm (2½in) on the side edges and 15cm (5½in) along the base hem and press. Mitre each base corner and secure it with slip stitch. Pin, tack and herringbone stitch along the side and base hems using matching thread.

③ Place the curtain fabric flat with the wrong side facing and mark the vertical centre line down the length of the fabric using a metre ruler and tailor's chalk. Mark lines 30cm (12in) apart on either side of

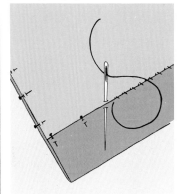

the centre line. With the wrong sides facing, centre the lining over the curtain fabric with the raw edges matching the top, side and hem edges of the curtain fabric. Pin the lining and curtain fabric

together along the central marked line.

④ Fold back the lining against the pins and lock stitch it to the fabric down the centre line, using matching thread. Begin stitching 10cm (4in) from the top raw edge and continue to within 2cm (¾in) of the fabric hem. Repeat this along each marked line, working outwards from the centre in each direction.

⑤ Pin and tack the lining and curtain fabric together along the top raw edge. Turn in 2cm (¾in) down the side edges of the lining and 5cm (2in) along the base edge. Press and pin the turned edges.

⑥ Slip stitch the lining to the curtain fabric along the side and base edges, using matching thread and small stitches. Finish the curtain in the same way as for an unlined curtain, turning down the top edges of the lining and curtain fabric together.

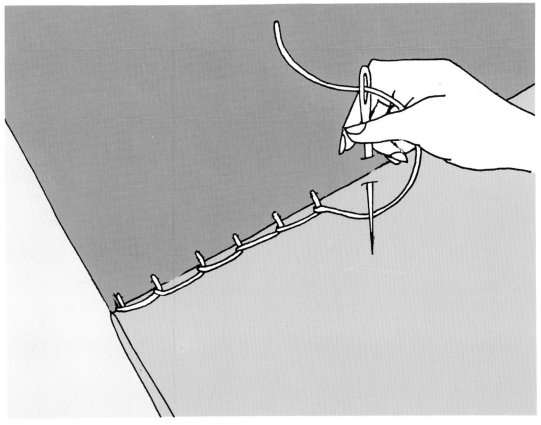

CAFE CURTAINS

CAFE CURTAINS

Café curtains are short, decorative curtains which are usually fixed halfway down the window. They can be made from a sheer fabric in the same way as an unlined curtain, but using a lightweight standard heading tape. A more decorative finish is to make one flat, ungathered curtain with a scalloped top and attach it to a pole with curtain rings.

① Cut out the fabric to the required size and then make the curtain up as for an ordinary unlined curtain, allowing an extra 1.5cm (⅝in) at the top and leaving the top edge unfinished. Divide up the width of the top edge to ascertain the number of finished scallops it will hold. 8cm (3in) scallops with 2cm (¾in) bands between each one are usual, with wider end bands.

② Make a paper pattern of the scalloped edge, as shown, and use it to mark the position of the scallops with tailor's chalk on to the wrong side of the curtain top, 1.5cm (⅝in) from the raw edge. Divide the remaining fabric into two equal parts for the end bands.

③ Cut out a facing 3cm (1¼in) wider than the curtain and 6.5cm (2⅝in) deeper than the scallops. Turn under 1.5cm (⅝in) along the base and side edges of the facing and press. Place the facing against the curtain with the right sides together and the curtain uppermost. Pin, tack and stitch along the marked line.

④ Cut out the scallop shapes 5mm (¼in) outside the stitched line. Trim corners and clip seam allowance at curves. Press and turn the facing through to the wrong side, gently pushing out the corners of the bands with the point of a knitting needle so that they are really square. Slip stitch the sides and base edge of the facing to the curtain.

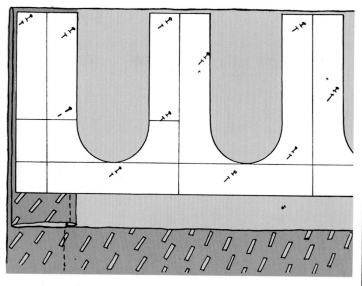

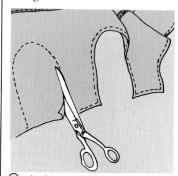

⑤ Blanket stitch a curtain ring to the centre of each band along the curtain and slide the rings on to the pole.

ACETATE - DUVETS

MACHINE-STITCHED HEM – SET SQUARES

CREDITS

The photographs on these pages have been reproduced by courtesy of the following: